Mary Flowers Braswell received her Ph.D. from Emory University, where her interests in literature, art history, and historical theology taken her to France and England to study both architecture and penitential documents. Previous publications include articles on Chaucer, William Langland, the *Pearl*-Poet, and the methodology of teaching English. She is a recipient of a 1982-83 grant from the National Endowment for the Humanities and is presently at work on a book about women in the Middle Ages. She is associate professor of medieval literature at the University of Alabama in Birmingham.

The Medieval Sinner

The Medieval Sinner

Characterization and Confession in the Literature
of the English Middle Ages

Mary Flowers Braswell

Rutherford • Madison • Teaneck
Fairleigh Dickinson University Press
London and Toronto: Associated University Presses

© 1983 by Associated University Presses, Inc.

PR
275
.S56
B7
1983

Associated University Presses, Inc.
4 Cornwall Drive
East Brunswick, N. J. 08816

Associated University Presses, Ltd.
27 Chancery Lane
London WC2A 1NF, England

Associated University Presses
2133 Royal Windsor Drive
Unit 1
Mississauga, Ontario, Canada L5J 1K5

Library of Congress Cataloging in Publication Data

Braswell, Mary Flowers, 1943–
    The Medieval sinner.

    Bibliography: p.
    Includes index.
    1. English literature—Middle English, 1100–1500—
History and criticism.   2. Sin in literature.   3. Confession
in literature.   4. Penance in literature.
5. Christian literature, English—History and criticism.
6. Penitentials.   I. Title.
PR275.S56B7   1982   820'.9'3520692   81-69040
ISBN 0-8386-3117-7

Printed in the United States of America

To John
and *in memoriam* Anne Amari Perry

Contents

Acknowledgments

I am indebted to so many people for making this book possible. My warmest thanks to Dr. Frederick Conner and to Dr. Robert Detweiler for encouraging me at an early and crucial stage of my career; to my friends at Emory University for providing me with a challenging academic atmosphere in which to work; to Ms. Antoinette Maggiore and Ms. Dana Davidson for typing and retyping various drafts of the manuscript; and to Mr. William Brooks and Mr. Richard A. Peacock for proofreading the manuscript for me. I am grateful to the University of Alabama in Birmingham for providing me with a faculty research grant that enabled me to spend time in the British Library in the summer of 1980. I owe a special debt to two of my professors: Dr. Thomas W. Lyman, for generously giving of his time to read and comment on various versions of this work, and Dr. John M. Bugge, my friend and mentor, for his patience, his astute critical guidance, and for first communicating to me a love for the Middle Ages. And, finally, I am indebted to my family: to my mother, Mary, for her encouragement along the way, and to my husband, John, without whose support and unceasing good humor this book would not have been written.

Introduction

There was once a woman who had committed many sinful acts but had confessed them all. However, a certain sin was of such magnitude that she was ashamed to tell it and hid it inside her. One day she came upon a friar who agreed to shrive her, and she told him of all her misdeeds save this dreadful one. But the friar was aware that she was withholding something from him, and he comforted her and encouraged her to tell all. Persuaded, she agreed to confess completely, and the words of the sin came flying out of her, each one blacker than pitch.[1]

A certain young canon lived a sinful life of incontinence and delight. One day he became sick, was shriven, received the last rites, and died. Within a few days after his death, he appeared to a friend and related that he was damned, for, even though he had confessed, he had withheld one important part of the sacrament—contrition. He had attested his sorrow to the priest, but his conscience had said to him: "what & I mend, I sall fall vnto syn agayn'; ffor my harte more declynyd vnto þat þan not for to syn."[2]

In the *Lives of the Fathers*, there is the tale of a holy hermit named Paul who could read men's thoughts and tell whether they were on the side of good or evil. He stood in the doorway of the church and saw many enter who were surrounded by good angels, but one man came who was dark and gloomy and who was led hither and thither by a bridle pulled by devils. The hermit prayed for the unhappy man, who was then converted. Rushing to the hermit, he revealed that he had for a long time "lyued in

11

fornicacion." Because of the hermit's prayers, however, he felt contrition and great sorrow and vowed to forsake all his "stynkynge synnes."[3]

These three exempla, from *Handlyng Synne*, the *Alphabet of Tales*, and the *Speculum Sacerdotale*, concern a character who emerged in the late Middle Ages whose advent was to change the nature of fiction for the next several hundred years. The woman who refused to confess completely, the lustful canon who confessed without being contrite, the man led by devils who was aided by the holy hermit to forsake his evil ways—these characters are all sinners. Unlike the saints and the questers for the Holy Grail, the sinner is concerned with matters of this world and those things which are forbidden to him. Unlike the antagonist, with whom he necessarily shares certain distinctive features, the sinner alone came to possess a real knowledge of sin—its definitions, its causes, and its circumstances—and he was able to articulate these things with a depth of motive and a self-awareness that his predecessors and contemporaries did not possess. The sinner was born of a more educated concept of man, his frailties and his limitations, which had evolved for centuries, and which culminated in the Fourth Lateran Council of 1215 and the decree of mandatory confession.

In his book *The Individual in Twelfth-Century Romance*, Robert W. Hanning points out the uniqueness of the protagonist in the chivalric romances of the last half of the twelfth century (1165–95). In these works, Hanning sees a character possessed of what he calls *engin*—that quality which allows the hero to manipulate and control situations within a literary work and to learn and grow as the story line progresses. According to Hanning, this individuality disappeared in the thirteenth century as society became more institutionalized, art more mannered, and liturgical observances more allegorized, and after the Fourth Lateran Council "codified" confessional practice and the emphasis on contrition. The "moment of inner openness to God's love that individualized the penitent's experience" in twelfth-century romance gave way to the

systematic interrogation of the confessional.[4] The reformed penitent is never an individual, but a type. His
confession has stripped him of those particular sins which
have made him unique, and he has espoused the cardinal
virtue of humility. His is a passive good; the goal of the
confessional has been met, and we find him interesting
not for his future activities but for his past.

But until the confession is ended, until the priest has
issued his order that the penitent go and sin no more, the
sinner stands alone. Isolated from his environment, his
will at odds with the Divine Will, he is an individual indeed. And his personality is composed of those *particular*
sins which he has committed in his own inimitable way.
While he remains sinful, he is possessed of a special kind
of *engin* and is able both to affect the fates of others and to
manipulate literary plots. And because a knowledge of sin
necessitates an inner awareness, his internal nature is as
important as his external one. He is a lively, rounded
character, unacceptable to the Church but attractive both
to modern readers and to those sinners in the medieval
audience who were able to view him in a very special way.

This study is concerned with the emergence and development of the sinner, first in the literature of the thirteenth century, then in the belletristic writers of the fourteenth century, primarily the "Ricardian poets"—
Langland, Gower, the *Pearl*-poet, and Chaucer.[5] These
poets learned a "psychology of sin" from the confessional,
for the long, intense scrutiny of penitent by priest taught
that penitent the advisability of self-awareness, and he
began to examine the "entente" behind his deeds. Poets
went to confession, too, and they put their knowledge to
work in the creation of sinful characters. Of crucial importance to the penitent is the one who hears his sins, who
can "grope tendrely a conscience in shrift."[6] So like his
counterpart in reality, the fictional sinner is always provided with some character who serves as his confessor,
generally a priest in the earlier works, but later on a lay
figure whose function can be determined by the appropri-
ateness of the words he speaks and the responses he

elicits from others. But before either of these characters could exist, the psychology of the confessional had to be formulated and the doctrine of sin made available to all.

It was not until the early thirteenth century that confession was made mandatory and the confessional process described above could come into being. The twenty-first canon of the Fourth Lateran Council of 1215, known as the *Omnis utriusque sexus* decree, required all the faithful to confess their sins to their own parish priest at least once a year at Easter time. Up to this point, penance had been voluntary, and neither the specific act of confession nor the presence of the priest was necessary for forgiveness of sins. Until the sixth century and sometimes thereafter in the continental West, it was public, and it was often humiliating. In early Christian times, the guilty one was required to wear goatskin or sackcloth and ashes, to fast, and to bewail his sins before the congregation. Often he was ostracized from the community and his social activities were curtailed for the remainder of his life. Furthermore, in the early centuries a person was allowed only one formal repentance for sins during his lifetime. If he sinned thereafter, he was perpetually damned. Evidently this philosophy of penance was not acceptable to the faithful, for since it was voluntary it was largely ignored. In the sixth century, the Celtic Church introduced private penance, and thereafter the emphasis fell on the act of confession itself. The Celts originated the confessional manuals that would prove to be enormously influential throughout the Middle Ages. Yet this system, too, was voluntary, and the majority chose to ignore it.

The situation changed in the thirteenth century when Pope Innocent III, in an effort to combat heresy and purify the Church, made annual confession mandatory. The repercussions were great. Neither clergy nor laity were prepared to meet the new responsibilities suddenly thrust upon them. Many theological problems emerged and demanded immediate attention. One result was to set in motion an educational program of massive proportions designed to refine man's conscience and to make him increasingly aware of his sins.

Although the Fourth Lateran Council ordered mandatory confession for all the Catholic world, it is the purpose of this book to examine the effects of this decree only in England, where a unique situation existed. King John was in perpetual conflict with the pope, and when the former refused to accept the appointment of Stephen Langton to the See of Canterbury, Innocent retaliated by placing England under an interdict that was to last for six years, three months, and three days. Though the economic growth of the country flourished during that time, the spiritual growth was severely retarded. Mass, save at a few conventual churches, was practically nonexistent, and the only sanctioned church services were the baptism of infants and the hearing of the confessions of the dying. It is safe to assume that, during these years, the particulars of the Mass were largely forgotten by most Englishmen; prelates would have had no clerics to train; and confession, which was a voluntary act, would have ceased to exist, though perhaps the more scrupulous would have confessed to one another. Because of this political situation, Monsignor Richard le Poore and the other English bishops returning from the Fourth Lateran Council would have had essentially to start afresh in educating the people so that they would be able to take full advantage of their confessions. It is no doubt for this reason that, in England alone, confession was required three times a year, rather than only once.[7]

To assist with this enormous task, thirteenth-century England produced a substantial amount of educational literature on the subject of penance—confessional manuals, synodalia, sermons, and the like—which is the subject of chapter 2. Only a portion of this material is extant, but from what does exist it is possible to determine the prevailing attitudes toward penance, and to infer particular sentiments toward moral behavior that were to affect the way fourteenth-century English literature achieved characterization. Certain ideas recur with regularity, such as emphasis on the contrition and humility of the penitent, detailing of degrees of sinfulness, and investigation of circumstances surrounding the sin.

The belletristic literature of the second half of the fourteenth century reflects these attitudes toward sin. By then, annual confession had been enforced in England for one hundred and fifty years, and the greater poets of the day and their audiences had thoroughly assimilated its tenets. Chapters 3 and 4 illustrate this process of assimilation in the works of William Langland, John Gower, the *Pearl*-poet, and Geoffrey Chaucer. These poets were in part concerned with the mechanics of the confessional and what those mechanics could reveal about the various mental states of the sinner. Their understanding of penance enabled them to create characters possessed of a considerable depth and complexity. And the ideas and idiom of the confessional manuals supplied them with guidelines for fashioning the personalities of the fictional sinners and the confessors (or laymen) who draw their sins from them. Thus, there is a previously unexplored cohesiveness among the writers of this era and among the sinners they create. But the stamp of the individual poet's art has, at the same time, transformed each character and made him unique.

The Medieval Sinner

1
The Genealogy of the Sinner:
A Study in the Background of Penance

On an April evening long ago, a blustery Harry Bailly convenes an assorted lot of pilgrims who have come together in his tavern and offers to guide them on their way to Canterbury. He explains the conditions under which he will lead them to the shrine of Becket at his "owene cost" (*almost*—he stands to gain at the journey's end) and instructs them quite clearly on their obligations for storytelling along the way. Throughout the journey he listens carefully to the tales he has initiated, encouraging and criticizing, eliciting "sentence" and "solaas." All too soon the pilgrims have told their tales—the Wife, the Merchant, the Canon's Yeoman, the Pardoner—the Parson has finished his "myrie tale in prose," and Chaucer has retracted his finest work. Within the framework described above, only the Parson's Tale seems properly "penitential." Few of the pilgrims themselves—the Knight, the Parson, and the Plowman are exceptions—could even be described as "devout." There are indeed sinners present in the group, but they are hardly contrite, and the often-heard voice of Harry Bailly is frequently obtuse, rambunctious, and rude. It is difficult to see how Chaucer's *Canterbury Tales* bears more than a superficial resemblance to such works as *Handlyng Synne* and the *Speculum Sacerdotale*; but behind the stories of the Canterbury pilgrims, and the works of Langland, Gower, and the *Pearl*-poet as well, lies a complicated mass of theological doctrine and ritual that had begun to evolve centuries before Chaucer's time, and that converged in the decree of mandatory confession in 1215.

The earliest Christian penance was not obligatory; it did not require a confession, nor did it involve a priest.[1] Throughout the patristic period (through A.D. 450), the Church was more concerned with the outer show of sorrow than with any inner changes that might have taken place as a result of sin. Penitents were often treated as criminals[2] and required to wear sackcloth and ashes or sometimes a special garb of goatskin to indicate that they were not lambs of God. They were to pray loudly and bewail their sins, and to be watched constantly by the elders of the congregation until a special ceremony reconciled them with the Church.[3] Early offenders were tried by the episcopal courts and ostracized by their peers, and they often faced poverty and exile. Moreover, the doctrine of the *paenitentia una* was in effect in the continental West until the sixth century. According to its dictates, one was allowed formal repentance for sins only once in a lifetime—after baptism. This posed a problem: if one had repented in good faith, but slipped and sinned again, how could he atone? He could not. The solution was foreseeable: he simply postponed baptism and penance until the end of his life. Penance, then, had lost its *raison d'être* and had become a preparation for death in old age. Such a system was harsh. By concentrating on externals, it ignored the motives and feelings of the individual. It is not surprising that this system was not a workable one, or that volunteers were few. As Saint Ambrose lamented in the fourth century, it was easier to find a man who had preserved his innocence than one who had properly performed his penance.[4]

But by the sixth century in the British Isles, a penitential system of an entirely different type had been developed by the Celtic Church that would ultimately resolve many of the issues raised in the patristic period. The method that the Celtic monks devised was quite different from that which existed on the continent.[5] Confession by the penitent, though still not required, was presupposed, and it assumed a certain prescribed form. The priest was now elevated to an important role, because it was he who guided the confessant through an enumeration of sins. Acts of penance were performed in private; there was no doctrine of the *paenitentia una* (in fact, frequent penance was urged); and, most important for present purposes, emphasis was placed on the motives and circumstances of the individual sinner.

The great importance attached to the act of confession is clearly illustrated by the handbooks of penance for- mulated by the monks that survive from the sixth through the eighth centuries. Consisting largely of lists of ques- tions designed to prompt confession of various sins, and of appropriate penances for those sins, these early works were intended primarily for use by priests. The lists were to be read aloud to the confessant—another priest or sometimes a layman—and the often formidable Latin translated for him if necessary.[6] These handbooks contain instructions for both priest and penitent on how to carry out their duties. The seventh-century *Penitential of Cum- mean*, for example, classifies confession as the fifth of seven ways of bringing health to a diseased soul. Further, it reminds the priest to be constantly aware of the attitude of his penitent, to observe carefully "the length of time anyone remains in his faults; with what learning he is instructed; with what passion he is assailed; with what courage he stands; with what tearfulness he is driven to sin."[7] Although the vow of secrecy taken by the priest did not become Canon Law until 1215, evidence indicates that such secrecy was already common practice in Ireland.[8]

Many of the Celtic penitentials reveal an attempt on the part of the Church to adapt the punishment to the indi- vidual sinner or to take into consideration the motive be- hind the deed. In the *Penitential of Cummean*, for instance, an adult thief is given a lengthy penance, but a boy "of ten years who steals anything shall do penance for seven days" (*MHP*, p. 102). The sixth-century *Penitential of Fin- nian* outlines the penance for one who has "intended fornication or murder, since the deed did not complete the intention, he has, to be sure, sinned in his heart; but if he quickly does penance, he can be helped" (*MHP*, p. 88). In an eighth-century manual ascribed to the Venerable Bede, the punishment set for one who has committed slaughter depends entirely on the motive. He who kills a layman "with malice aforethought or for the possession of his inheritance" must do penance for four years. One who kills to avenge his brother is assigned penance for "three forty-day periods and the appointed days." And one who slays in public warfare does penance for only forty days (*MHP*, pp. 245–25).

The attitudes revealed in the Celtic penitentials may be seen as an early form of psychological therapy. In his edition of these works, John T. McNeil notes the humane intentions of the Celtic monks in their administering of penance. On a social level, a reformed penitent is free of censure. Unless his crime was a heinous one, he is not deprived of his rights as a citizen, and he is able to resume normal relationships with his family and friends. Clearly, the aim of the monks was to restore the penitent to harmony with his environment, with God, and with the Church. But we must note that, in being so restored, the penitent becomes once more a member of a group and loses his individuality as a sinner. McNeil's comments are significant: "Beyond the theological considerations [of Celtic penance], we see in the detailed prescriptions the objectives of an inward moral change, the setting up of a process of character reconstruction which involves the correction of special personal defects and the reintegration of personality" (p. 46). In correcting his "special personal defects," the sinner is directed, in effect, to divest himself of his ingenuity, to become humble and passive, to forsake his own private, egotistical battle. His individual personality is "reintegrated" into a *type*.

The "inward moral change" that takes place through the correct use of the confessional is of importance to us because it involves the internal development of the sinner. The very term *penitent* implies that some change is taking place. The sinner has become one who is sorry for his past actions and is willing to undertake a prescribed punishment for them. A reformed penitent is self-aware; his encounter with the priest has taught him something about himself, and he determines to make a change in his life: he will be "good." On a very elementary level he has learned what constitutes a sin, both in thought and in deed. His experience as a penitent will make him more conscious of future actions, and he will turn his attention from the things of this world to those of the next; like a sick man, he avoids that which once made him ill.[9]

It is not surprising that this Celtic system of penance with its private, repeatable character and its emphasis on man's inner nature became, with some modifications, the typical penance of medieval Europe. It was introduced to the monks on the Continent in the sixth century by Saint Columbanus and his companions, and one might well imagine that it was met with relief by the Continental brothers. Once this system was adopted, it remained relatively fixed for the next six hundred years. This did not mean, however, that major problems concerning the enforcement of regulations were not to emerge.

During the Carolingian period (750–1000), and well into the eleventh century, confession seems to have been less strictly enforced, despite attempts to appeal to the more mundane interests of the popular mind by alleging that it was a source of earthly good fortune.[10] A major obstacle in the way of successful penance was the penitentials themselves and the satisfaction that they assigned for various sins. Individual Celtic manuals lacked uniformity in the lengths of the penances required for a given sin. This did not seem to present a problem for the Celts, for their manuals were from widely differing localities and were composed over several hundred years. For the Franks, however, the possession of great numbers of these books caused confusion. Compilers saw contradictions in them, and they could not resist writing down one after another the inconsistencies that they saw. The tendency among penitents, naturally enough, was to select the easiest method of satisfaction. And because a system of commutations had rapidly developed that converted prayers into periods of time, many of the "penances" were not penances at all in the strict sense of the word. For example, a hundred protestations and a single Confiteor were equal to a day's penance. One "King Edgar" decreed that it was sufficient merely to have a great fear—*un "grand" peur*—for three days to equal penance for seven years![11] The discrepancies in these Carolingian penitentials were compounded by their uncertain origin. Fraudulent manuals appeared, claiming authorship by Columbanus or Bede, and this undermined the authority of all the manuals. It is understandable that the reformers of the ninth century wanted to abolish these books altogether and to reinstate the harsh ancient penalties.[12] The interior probing of the Celtic manuals and consequently the emphasis on the *individual* sinner had vanished almost without a trace.

In their place, penitentials commonly called "tariffs" evolved. Little is known about them, but it seems that they were simply lists (hence the name) of the various sins that could be committed and a corresponding list of penances that applied automatically to them—prayers and genuflections for lesser sins and hard fasting for greater ones, for example. A penitent would enumerate his sins to a priest, and in turn the priest would read the equivalent satisfaction from the list, guided by the maxim "public penance for public sins and private penance for private sins."[13] It is easy to see that such a mechanical system of confession, in which the publicity the sin had received was of more consequence than the act itself, would not reveal the motives and circumstances of the sin or of the sinner. Yet, mechanical as they were, these tariffs were to prevail until the beginning of the thirteenth century, when a type of manual that was to prove of considerable importance later on—the *Liber Poenitentiales* of Bartholomew of Exeter, Alain de Lille, Raymond de Peñafort, and especially of Robert of Flamborough—would usher in a new tradition and Pope Innocent III would convene the Fourth Lateran Council and make confession mandatory for all.

Pope Innocent did not assemble his council without good reason.[14] A shrewd canon lawyer, he was well aware of problems that beset the Church from all sides and confident that he could deal with them. For some time a number of heretical sects had presented a problem for the pope. The Albigensians, who preached against the death and resurrection of Christ, hell, and purgatory, had become especially strong in northern Italy, southern France, and throughout the province of Languedoc and were gaining converts from the Catholic faith. Moreover, corruption was rampant not only among the laity but also among the clergy, who openly engaged in such immoral acts as war, concubinage, and simony. As the canons of the council reveal, most of these men were illiterate and unable to perform Mass correctly. Many drank excessively and engaged in trade to supplement their incomes. The laity (though we have no reason to believe that their actions were in any way superior) were justified in mistrusting these "spiritual guides." And although the necessity of the priest in the penitential system had been established in the ninth century, this position now came into question. Would it not be more satisfactory to confess to God or to a layman than to a sinful priest? The Fourth Lateran Council directed itself to these problems.

In some ways, the council was not a revolutionary one. A number of its seventy canons were simply a reissue of those of previous ecumenical conferences which had not been carried into effect; others were no more than a formalizing of certain beliefs and customs that were already vaguely held or practiced. The majority are concerned with reparation—making amends for wrongdoing—and the specific details they contain paint a vivid picture of ecclesiastical ills in the Middle Ages. Most of the canons, however, were not to have lasting effect.

This is not true of the twenty-first canon, the *Omnis utriusque sexus* decree, which has been called "the most important legislative act in the history of the Church."[15] This decree would prove to be the climax of hundreds of years in the development of the penitential system. For the first time it had the authority of the pope and his council, and Innocent had reinforced his order by Canon Law. One was no longer free to choose whether he wished to partake in the sacrament of penance; it was now imposed on every Christian as a duty.[16] The ordinance begins by stating unequivocally,

> Omnis utriusque sexus fidelis, postquam ad annos discretionis pervenerit, omnia sua solus peccata confiteatur, fideliter, saltem semel in anno, proprio sacerdoti, & injunctam sibi pœnitentiam studeat pro viribus adimplere, suscipiens reverenter ad minus in Pascha eucharistiæ sacramentum: nisi forte de consilio proprii sacerdotis, ob aliquam rationabilem causam ad tempus ab ejus perceptione duxerit abstinendum: alioquin & vivens ab ingressu ecclesiae arceatur, & moriens Christiana careat sepultura. Unde hoc salutare statutum frequenter in ecclesiis publicetur, ne quisquam ignorantiæ cæcitate velamen excusationis assumat. Si quis autem alieno sacerdoti voluerit justa de causa sua confiteri peccata, licentiam prius postulet & obtineat proprio sacerdote, cum aliter ille ipse non possit solvere, vel ligare.[17]

> [All the faithful of both sexes, after they have reached the age of discretion, must confess all their sins at least once a year, to their own parish priest, and perform to the best of their abilities the penance imposed, reverently receiving the sacrament of the Eucharist at least on Easter Sunday, unless by chance he (the priest) should counsel their abstaining from its reception. Otherwise they shall be cut off from the Church during their lifetime and shall be without a Christian burial in death. Whereupon let this salutary statute frequently be made in public in churches, lest anyone may assume by blind ignorance a veil of excuse. However, if anyone with a just cause should wish to confess his sins to another parish priest, let him first seek and obtain permission from his own parish priest, since otherwise that one cannot loose or bind (the penitent).]

By this decree the Church not only affirmed its authority; it also gained control of the individual conscience. Several aspects of this canon warrant examination in detail.

First, the faithful, after reaching the "age of discretion,"[18] are advised that they should "confess all their sins at least once a year." The word *sin* in this case normally refers to mortal sins, all of which must be acknowledged. Although full allowance was to be made for the imperfections of the human memory, it was soon apparent that there was less to fear from forgetfulness than from conscious suppression by the unwilling penitent. Such suppression would cause an invalid confession, a mortal sin. Anticipating problems of this nature, the council was careful to advise the priest that part of his duty as a confessor lay in the diligent investigation into all circumstances of sin.

To aid the priest in this inquiry, old penitentials were updated, resembling the Celtic manuals in their minuteness and their personal nature, but marked by an increasing demand for thoroughness. To this end, the new English penitentials, unlike the Celtic manuals, often indicate the exact words the priest was to say to the penitent and include paradigms of ways the confessant might be expected to respond. When the concept of mandatory confession fell under the scrutiny of scholastic commentators, the number of possible sins increased enormously, along with the differentiation in their grades and varieties.[19] This may suggest a practical reason for requiring confession only once annually, for the exhaustiveness of these penitential manuals indicates that the overworked priest would need several hours to interrogate each penitent. Nevertheless, confessions of devotion—those made freely—were encouraged by the Church for the spirituality of the individual.

Still, many a sinner would not have made his annual confession had he not been motivated by the fear of eternal damnation. Gruesome portrayals of hell on the west portal of many a cathedral reminded him of what lay in store for the unrepentant. Furthermore, if he did not confess, he was not eligible to receive the sacrament of the Eucharist. Thereupon, he was excommunicated and shunned by the faithful. Upon death, he was denied a Christian burial, which precluded future resurrection.

To insure the penitent a proper confession, the *Omnis*

utriusque sexus decree provided guidelines for the priest. He was advised to be "discreet and cautious," but at the same time to inquire carefully into the circumstances of the sinner and the sin—*diligenter inquirens & peccatoris circumstantias & peccati*—so that he might know what to advise for each individual situation. A fourteenth-century confessional manual says of these duties,

> Prest aght be skilful soft & meke.
> knawande riʒtwise loueli in speke.
> & quat shrift to him is knawen.
> he laine hit lelli as his awen.
> skilful to knaw þe pliʒt.
> quilc is heui & quilk is liʒt.
> & nameli knaw þe circumstaunce.
> þat mesours of siþe our penaunce.[20]

To judge wisely, the priest must secure enough detail from the sinner to classify the sin accurately. But he is warned throughout the thirteenth and fourteenth centuries to be prudent in his interrogation and compassionate for the plight of the sinner; and, lest a too-stringent penance go unheeded, the priest is advised to be merciful. The dire fate of the rigorous confessor is illustrated in the *Alphabet of Tales* (p. 128, ll. 3–17): a would-be penitent confessed to a priest and a pope, who were so strict in their penances that he killed them both. Finally, he found a third confessor who "hard hym mekelie & spak frendlie vnto him" (l.11) and assigned him one very small penance that he was able to carry out. If any truth lay behind this story, a confessor would have been wise to take heed.

In addition to amassing details about the sins themselves, the confessor was instructed by the Fourth Lateran Council to ask the penitent what parish he was from and to require him to confess to his own parish priest or to gain permission if he wished to go to another. And, finally, the confessor was to take a specific vow of secrecy, which forbade him to reveal any of the mortal sins revealed to him in the confessional, either specific or generic, as well as specific venial sins. Secrecy is mentioned in the Celtic

penitentials, but it was not until the Fourth Lateran Council that "the seal of confession" became Canon Law.

The Church, then, had made its position offical regarding mandatory confession to a priest. But it is important to
note that the concept of the layman as confessor died
hard. *De vera et falsa poenitentia,* a popular work falsely
attributed to Saint Augustine, stated that the penitent
would receive more forgiveness if he confessed to several
different persons, and confession to laymen became popular in the case of venial sins.[21] Aquinas had also stated that
in certain cases one might confess to a layman.[22] And as
late as the fourteenth century, the Synod of Cahors stated
that a dying person might confess to any man or woman
handy. These laymen had no power to forgive sins, but
their services enabled the priest to absolve the penitent
after his death.[23] The fourteenth-century *Clensyng of
Mannes Soule* says of this notion that if a man is in "greet
perel" of his soul and can find no priest,

> he may be confessid to a lewid man: *and*
> al be it þat a lewid man þat is no preest.
> may not asoile / ȝitt for as myche as he
> knowlechiþ to his neiȝbore þe filþe of
> his synne in desire to haue a preest:
> þerfore he shal haue forȝeu[en]esse. but
> *not* so soone come out of peyne. as if he
> were confessid to a preest / .[24]

The *Omnis utriusque sexus* decree was to effect a momen-
tous change in the history of the Church. Innocent III was
by no means blind to its potential; yet it is difficult to
believe that even he could have foreseen what enormous
control this canon was to give to the Church in establishing its authority over the conscience of every believer.
Because penance was now a prerequisite for the Eucharist,
the most important of the sacraments, its satisfactory performance was essential to the well-being of every Christian. Penance had become "a compulsory test of fitness for
a share in the full membership of the Church, without

which man was debarred from the hope of eternal salvation."[25]

It is not surprising that the twenty-first decree of the Lateran Council met with obstacles and foot-dragging or that problems that could have remained hidden as long as penance was voluntary suddenly emerged as soon as the sacrament became mandatory. The canons of the council graphically portray the thirteenth-century priest "spending half of the night in banqueting and in unlawful gossip," saying Mass "scarcely four times a year," or not attending Mass at all. From a practical standpoint, there were not enough priests to provide for the needs of the people who would require their services. Friars who were called upon to help administer the sacrament soon found themselves engaged in cold war with the regular clergy, who were jealous of their competition. Most important was the ignorance of both laity and clergy, who needed to be taught the ramifications of all the mortal sins in a way that they could understand. But before this could take place, such important aspects of the doctrine of penance as intent, motive, will, and contrition—crucial to an understanding of the mind of the sinner—needed thorough analysis. This task was left to the analytical minds of the thirteenth-century Schoolmen.

The role of intention in the act of sinning was of primary concern for the Schoolmen, for a sin could be mortal only if it were committed according to the design of the sinner. It could not occur accidentally. The intellect must first perceive and judge the morality of the act, and then the will must freely consent to engage in it. This period of reflection precedes all grave sins and is sinful within itself, for one may be judged according to those sins he planned to carry out whether he actually performed them or not. The awareness of the individual, therefore, is essential to the sinful act.

Not only the intention of the action but also the motive behind it was necessary for an understanding of sin. Though this idea of motive could be found in the Bible, in Aristotle's *Nicomachean Ethics,* and in Augustine, it had reached its zenith before the Fourth Lateran Council in the twelfth-century works of Peter Abelard.[26] In the *Ethics*, Abelard explains his theory of intention and sin. Acts in themselves are neutral; only their agents can supply them with morality. If one does something that has the form of sin, but does it out of innocence or ignorance or believes in his heart that it is right, then he commits no intended fault and is not guilty of an evil deed.

> Solum quippe animum in remuneratione boni uel mali, non effecta operum, Deus adtendit, ne quid de culpa uel de bona uoluntate nostra proueniat pensat, sed ipsum animum in pro- posito suae intentionis, non in effectu exterioris operis, diiudicat. Opera quippe quae, ut prediximus, eque reprobis ut electis communia sunt, omnia in se indifferentia sunt nec nisi pro intentione agentis bona uel mala dicenda sunt, non uidelicet quia bonum uel malum sit ea fieri, sed quia bene uel male fiunt, hoc est, ea intentione qua conuenit fieri, aut minime.

> [God considers only the mind in rewarding good or evil, not the results of deeds, and he thinks not of what comes forth from fault or from our good but judges the mind itself in the design of its intention, not in the outcome of an outward deed. Works in fact, which as we have previously said are common to the damned and the elect alike, are all indifferent in themselves and should be called good or bad only on ac- count of the intention of the agent, not, that is, because it is good or bad for them to be done but because they are done well or badly, that is, by that intention by which it is or is not fitting that they should be done.][27]

The same act can result in varying merit. For instance, the delivering up of the Son was an act performed by God, Christ, and Judas. But the merit was not the same for each one. The motive of God and Christ was good, but that of Judas was evil.

> Nec in opere sed in intentione meritum operantis uel laus consistit. Sepe quippe idem a diuersis agitur, per iusticiam unius et per nequitiam alterius, ut si unum reum duo sus-

pendant, ille quidem zelo iusticiae, hic antiquae odio inim-
iciciae, et cum sit suspensionis eadem actio, et utique quod
bonum est fieri et quod iusticia exigit agant, per diuersitatem
tamen intentionis idem a diuersis fit, ab uno male, ab altero
bene.

[The merit or glory of the doer lies in the intention, not in the
deed. In fact the same thing is often done by different people,
justly by one and wickedly by another, as for example if two
men hang a convict, that one out of zeal for justice, this one
out of a hatred arising from an old enmity, and although it is
the same act of hanging and although they certainly do what
is good to do and what justice requires, yet, through the
diversity of their intention, the same thing is done by diverse
men, by one badly, by the other well. (Pp. 28–29)]

It is possible that Abelard's emphasis on the intent of
the individual sinner and on a very personal system of
justice in which the degree of guilt corresponds to the
underlying motive for the sin was a reaction to the crude
tariffs that figured in the penance of his day.[28] Their arbi-
trary nature simply assumed that all sinners were of a
common mind, and that one motive—the desire to do
evil—was behind every sin. But Abelard is also a
"nominalist"—the particular, individual thing is for him
the reality. The idea that man is a free individual, both a
part of humanity and separate from it, permeates all his
work and greatly influenced the later Middle Ages.

Like Abelard, Saint Thomas Aquinas saw the distinction
between deed and intention as a test of deliberateness in
judging the degree of guilt in mortal sin. In the *Summa
Theologiae*, Aquinas notes that all sins are not equal.
Habitual sins are greater, for example, but the sin for
which the impulse is very great is less grave than that sin
for which the impulse is weak. Just as all sins are not
equal, so are all motives for sinning not equal, for different
sins have different motives: "just as the motive in the sin
of intemperance is love for bodily pleasures, while the
motive of the sin of insensibility is hatred of the same."[29]
A single sin may have different motives:

for instance that a man eat hastily may be due to the fact that he cannot brook the delay in taking food, on account of the rapid exhaustion of the digestive humours; and that he desire too much food, may be due to a naturally strong digestion; that he desire choice meats is due to his desire for pleasure in taking food. Hence in such matters, the corruption of different circumstances entails different species of sins.[30]

Therefore, an act should not be judged within itself, but only in light of the motives behind it or the circumstances that caused it to be.

The concern with the mind of the sinner sinning led naturally to a consideration of will. Defined by the Schoolmen as man's "faculty of choice," it is perhaps this act of volition that most clearly differentiates the saint from the sinner. The will of every true Christian is inclined toward the Divine Will, or the *bonum in communis*. And once it espouses this common good, it ceases striving for those things forbidden to it. The sinner, on the other hand, shuns the common good for his own *individual* good—he is an egotist; therefore he chooses evil, and, in doing so, he isolates himself from those around him. One might choose evil for a variety of reasons: he might be preoccupied with self or in an emotional state particularly conducive to evil. An angry or terrified man, for example, is distracted from his use of moral knowledge. But sins that derive neither from passion nor from ignorance are the product of a will deliberately prepared to choose evil and are therefore graver because they are caused by the disposition of the will.[31]

Along with intent, motive, and will, a major interest of the scholastic commentators was "contrition": the degree of sorrow a penitent expresses over his sins, the degree of detestation that he feels for them, and his firm resolve for amendment. Perfect contrition is sorrow springing from one's love for God and one's remorse for having offended Him. This is the ideal state, which immediately reconciles the sinner to God, but it is a state that few penitents can successfully achieve. Therefore, true sorrow can originate from other sources as well: fear of hell or of the loss of heaven; disgust with the filth of sin. These motives, provided that they are not accompanied by any love of sin and that the sinner sincerely desires a reconciliation with God, can also lead to absolution. This imperfect contrition, or "attrition," must be accompanied by works of charity.[32] Such a careful examination of the thought processes of the mind of the sinner—his motive, intent, will, and contrition—would be necessary for the penitent-priest relationship in the confessional, and it would lay the groundwork for the interior probing of character by fourteenth-century poets.

Such were the issues that occupied the best theological minds of the thirteenth century. The answers were complicated ones and there was much disagreement among individuals. But because penance was now mandatory, the properties of confession had to be workable, and they had to be made known. Thomas Aquinas summarized the major qualities as follows:

> Sit simplex, humilis confessio, pura, fidelis,
> Atque frequens, nuda, discreta, libens, verecunda,
> Integra, secreta, lacrymabilis, accelerata,
> Fortis et accusans, et sit parere parata.[33]

> [It must be a simple, humble confession, plain, faithful,
> And also frequent, revealing, discreet, liberating, modest,
> Complete, secret, sorrowful, swift,
> Courageous, and accusing, and it must prepare one to carry
>   out one's promises.]

In the next century, poets will transform these qualities of confession into aspects of character. The fictional character who evolves from the perfect penitent will be humble. He will be unconcerned with the gratification of his own personal desires and will focus always on God. He will confess his faults to one who elicits his sins and motives, who serves as his priest. His confession will be *simplex*, not glossed with fancy words, but it will also be *nuda*, revealing as much about his state of sinfulness as he knows. He will not be a habitual sinner, but instead will confess soon after the fault is committed, for he will know that time lived in sin is wasted. If the character is self-aware, he will express his sorrow for his misdeeds, for without true sorrow he cannot find true forgiveness. He will often explain his "entente," the motive behind his actions, and the circumstances surrounding his sin. His confession will be accusatory; he will place the blame on himself and not on someone else. And he will be fully intent on carrying out the promises made in the confessional and in completing the satisfaction assigned by the priest. Finally, and most important, if he is truly repentant, some character change will have taken place in the humble penitent in his firm resolve to mend his ways. No longer will he seek to control his environment; rather, he will be controlled by the Church. The character who flagrantly violates the qualities of the confession, however, will remain eternally the sinner. It is with this character that the remainder of this study is concerned.

2
Educating the Audience: The Sinner Emerges

When the Fourth Lateran Council adjourned, the bishops who had attended returned to their own countries to confront the *ignorantiæ cæcitate*—the blind ignorance—of the people. But educating priest and layman, and ultimately an entire English audience, was an assignment more complicated than these bishops could have known. To begin with, the vast majority of the people—including many priests—could not read. Most could not understand the Latin in which the literature of moral instruction was generally couched, and it is small wonder if both learned and unlearned profited little from Mass. Much is implied in the instruction books that warn priests that at least the *first* syllable of each Latin word must be said correctly.[1] Moreover, there were problems with vocabulary. Academic Latin had a vocabulary too limited to deal with passions, motives, and feelings, and as the thirteenth century progressed man found himself turning more and more to the vernacular.[2] But thirteenth-century English was too unsophisticated to sustain a depth of theme, and thus the topics it could deal with were limited also. The *Omnis utriusque sexus* decree helped bring about a change. Throughout the thirteenth century a great deal of catechetical literature was introduced to teach the uneducated priest, so that he might in turn instruct the laity. To overcome the language barrier, much of this literature—sermons and Mass books, for example—inevitably came to be written *populo vulgariter*, in English. And in order to deal adequately with matters of doctrine, the vernacular vocabulary necessarily expanded to include words needed to articulate attitudes about sin and the inner life. By the fourteenth century, words such as *intent* (i.e., motive), *guilt, confess, grope* (in the sense of investigating the conscience), and *repent* had seeped into the secular vocabulary,[3] making possible fictional characters possessed of these concepts. The interiority of Christianity, with its emphasis on what one feels in the heart, naturally gave way to the articulation of those inner feelings in the confessional, and subsequently to character analysis as well.

In analyzing the extant English penitential literature of the thirteenth century, one is struck by its conventional character. It might be said without exaggeration that authors avoided originality like a pestilence.[4] Therefore, certain ideas recur with regularity: the emphasis on the contrition of the penitent, for example, and on the exact nature of the sorrow that is felt; also the list of the seven deadly sins with their numerous offspring, often entailing a great degree of elaboration. Much importance is placed on the circumstances of sin—*quis, quid, ubi, per quos, quoties, cur, quomodo, quando*—by means of which priests could force penitents to search their own actions for motive. It is the orderliness of this literature that enables one to get a clear idea of the prevailing attitudes toward education in the confessional.

Late-twelfth-century England was marked by a continuation of the tariff books, essentially unchanged from the Carolingian period, which emphasized lists of sins and penances and deemphasized pastoral technique. Precouncil English theologians did not experiment with new types of manuals but instead turned their attention to the production of *Summae* and *Sentences* based on the works of Peter Lombard. Such penitential works as did appear did not significantly affect the thirteenth century and have scarcely been touched by later scholars.[5]

After the middle of the twelfth century, however, when penance had come to be regarded as a sacrament, the theology of confession began to undergo expansion and refinement. And in the early thirteenth century, for reasons that are unclear, the tariffs were abandoned. In their place emerged books of general principles whereby a priest could estimate the gravity of any sin confessed to him. By asking a series of very specific questions, he could discover the penitent's knowledge of his actions and the extent to which his will was involved. Thereby he could determine the degree of consent for each of the major sins. The *Omnis utriusque sexus* decree had stated that confessors should seek out *et peccatoris circumstantias et peccati* [both the circumstances of the sinner and of the sin itself]. The use of questions of circumstance, which were applicable to any given situation, enabled the priest to dispense with long lists of sins and, at the same time, to use the manual as an aid to understanding more clearly the mental disposition of the sinner with whom he dealt.

The earliest specimen of this type of confession manual is the *Liber Poenitentialis* of Robert of Flamborough, which exists in forty-three manuscripts and seems to have been written between 1208 and 1215. Robert's work was probably the first to make available to confessors in a short, comprehensive, and readable form the new Canon Laws, promoted by the Fourth Lateran Council, "organized in a practical way for solving cases of conscience."[6] It delves into pastoral psychology (a point to which I shall return later) by specifying that a confessor should have the heart of a reconciler, the just severity of a judge, and the mercy of a doctor of medicine.

The *Liber Poenitentialis* is divided into five books. Book I is concerned with the methods of receiving the penitent; Book II, with the laws governing matrimony; Book III, with ordination; Book IV, with the virtues and vices; and Book V, with the penances for the various sins. The format of the first four parts gives us a sample dialogue between priest and penitent. Still, it was not intended as a working manual actually to be used in confessions, but as a textbook for priests on the proper methods of interrogation. It is Books I and IV that are most pertinent to this discussion, because they show a penitent "learning" and revealing himself through dialogue. For although the penitent in the *Liber Poenitentialis* is a fictitious one, Robert endows him with some imaginary traits (however slight) that make him appear, within the pages of this manual, "realistic." He has certain distinctive features and a personality that is delineated by the penetrating investigation of the confessor. His specific qualities make this fictional penitent—and his priest—something of the prototype of those found in later medieval English literature.

Book I begins with the entrance of the penitent, who asks to be shriven even though he is a member of another diocese and needs permission. After determining that the penitent has been given the proper permission to be confessed elsewhere, the priest sets about to know this man's state of mind, for he was not to absolve any sinner whom he did not judge to be truly sorry for his sins. The *Liber Poenitentialis* opens with the attempts on the part of the priest to have the confessant articulate this sorrow and to teach him the qualities of the penitent: sorrow for the past, caution for the future, complete and honest confession. The penitent (Poenitens) immediately reveals his ignorance: *Non plane intelligo quid sit ista quatuor observare*[7] [I do not understand plainly what it means to observe those four conditions]. He is contrite but has not been able to abstain from sin in the past. The priest (the Sacerdos) promises to explain the sins one by one, and the Poenitens expresses his willingness to become a proselyte. The book ends with the Sacerdos preparing to begin his task.

In Book IV, the priest questions and instructs the penitent on the seven deadly sins, all of which this particular sinner seems to have committed at least once, though he often does not understand the exact definition of the offenses. This gives the confessor an opportunity to explain them to him so that Robert's clerical audience might learn also. The interchange of priest and penitent on the sin of pride, *superbia*, provides a typical example of the method used:

[SACERDOS]:   Superbia laborasti?
POENITENS: Quid est superbia?
SACERDOS: Superbire est super alios ire: quando ergo
              super alios te extollis, tunc superbis.
POENITENS: Frequenter hoc feci et ex consuetudine.
SACERDOS: Pete veniam et cessa de cetero.
POENITENS: Peto, domine, et per gratiam Dei cessabo de
              cetero. (P. 179)

[PRIEST: Are you suffering from pride?
PENITENT: What is pride?
PRIEST: To be proud is to go above others: when,
              therefore, you extol yourself above all others,
              then you are proud.
PENITENT: I do this frequently and from habit.
PRIEST: Beg forgiveness and leave off this thing.
PENITENT: I am sorry, Father, and by the grace of God, I
              will leave off this thing.]

It is no mere accident that the penitent's pride, his egotism, is the first sin to be attacked by the priest. For this sin
of self is the worst of all sins. Until one's self-image is
lowered, he cannot feel humility, a prime objective of the
confessional. The attitude of the Poenitens here—his
eagerness to repent and his promise that he will not be
proud again—is the first step toward lowering his self-
esteem. He will no longer "extol [himself] above all
others." Rather, he will put himself below them.

In its treatment of pride, this early confessional manual
reveals a technique found in the works of Langland, the
Pearl-poet, and especially John Gower. The priest begins
his investigation with a penitent who possesses much egotism, one who is devoted solely to his own self-interest.
Because the penitent is contrite and wants to change his
life, the priest can accuse him of all aspects of the major
sins, slowly turning the penitent away from self and toward God. But at the same time the penitent, when he
truly intends to sin no more, loses most of that which
makes him unique. The uniqueness of the individual soul,
of course, is of the essence of Christianity; but, from the
point of view of literary psychology, the kind of humility

the penitential system required of its penitents is at odds with individualism. In the selfless compliance of the individual will to God's will—the confirming of "[þe] wil be þe wil of god" (*Clensyng*, p. 148, 1. 6)—no room is left for the kind of assertive behavior that makes for effective literary characterization. A *selfless* individual possesses no traits that can be developed. Paradoxically, then, the reformed penitent can be an interesting literary character only in a retrospective way—we are interested in what he *did*, not what he *will* do—for the very egotism that fosters characterization is forbidden by the Church. The egotistical character can exist only so long as some part of him rebels against God's laws—so long as he remains a sinner.

When the priest has completed his interrogation of the sin of pride, he turns to *invidia*, or envy, asking the penitent:

> SACERDOS: Invidia laborasti? Ad indiviam [*sic*] pertinent ista: ingratitudo (accepti scilicet beneficii), malitia, invenio mali (scilicet quando scit homo invenire malitias, seditiones, nequitias), susurratio (scilicet quando scit homo spargere voces ambiguas et seminare inter fratres discordias), conjuratio, conspiratio, dissensio, schisma, suspicio, seditio, odium, exsultatio (scilicet de alienis malis), afflictio (de alienis scilicet bonis), detractio (tum loquendo tum, quod deterius est, audiendo), depravatio (cum dico "Iste multum orat, multum jejunat, multas facit eleemosynas," et tu respondes "Frater, hoc non facit pro Deo, sed quia ad illam vel illam aspirat dignitatem," deprevatio est); compressio est: cum dico "Iste bonus est," et tu respondes "Verum est, sed non ita bonus ut tu credis," compressio est; amaritudo (quando scilicet alii sunt in prosperitate, in felicitate, et amaricatur animus tuus; frequens est hoc in hominibus invenire). In aliquo istorum offendisti et tu de omnibus petis veniam et de cetero cavebis?

POENITENS: Peto, domine, et de cetero per gratiam Dei cavebo. (Pp. 180–81)

[PRIEST: Have you been afflicted with Envy? These things pertain to Envy: ingratitude (for instance, for a kindness received), malice, inventing evil (for example, when a man knows how to devise vices, dissensions, wantonnesses), tale-bearing (for example, when a man knows how to circulate doubtful words and to sow seeds of discord among brothers), plotting conspiracy, dissension, schism, suspicion, sedition, hatred, excessive rejoicing (for example, about other's bad fortunes), misery (for example, because of another's good fortune), detraction (first by speaking, then a thing that is more harmful, by listening), holding back (when I say, "That one prays much, fasts much, gives many alms," and you respond, "Father, he is not doing that for God, but because he wants this or that honor," that is holding back; it is holding back when I say, "That man is good," and you respond, "That is true, but he is not so good as you believe," it is holding back; bitterness (for example, when others are prosperous, happy, and your soul is embittered; this is frequently found in men). Have you offended in any of those things and will you be on guard against them?

PENITENT: I beg forgiveness, Father, and through the grace of God I will guard against all those things.]

By speaking or listening to harmful things, by plotting evil deeds or rejoicing when others are unhappy, the sinner guilty of *invidia* is simultaneously manipulating both events and people and separating himself from them. He is causing action (later on, plot) by his use of *engin*—by using his wits to set events in motion. On receiving a kindness, the envious man is ungracious; he delights in pitting friend against friend. In addition, envy is his stimulus for spreading false rumors and for stirring up dissension. Such a man is devious, his motives often at odds with his deeds. He is "good" in order to win honors; he pretends to be pious when he is not. In this portrayal, the envious man comes momentarily alive. His emotions and intentions can be analyzed, and he can be seen busily engaging in a sinful life. The Poenitens admits his familiarity with envy and promises to be on guard in the future.

After discussing each of the deadly sins, the confessor turns to the circumstances surrounding them. He begins by determining if the penitent guilty of lechery is also guilty of incest, and, if so, how close was the kin involved. He is asked if he has sexually molested a nun, or a virgin, or anyone in his family, from his godmother to his nephew. He is queried about the religion of the other party, if he or she be Jew or Gentile, infidel or heretic. And he is questioned about committing fornication in a sacred place, such as a church or cemetery, and is told how to make restitution. He is asked about his relationships with prostitutes, or if he has done "infamy" (here, trickery) in order to commit fornication, or if there are any other sins that he has not confessed. Finally, after a lengthy list of sins has come to an end, the priest sums up the character of the penitent as follows:

> Multas personas, et masculos et feminas, male aspexisti, concupivisti, sollicitasti, tractasti, osculatus es. Multa alia exciderunt tibi a memoria; multa sunt occulta tua; multae sunt omissiones tuae. Bona etiam quae fecisti minus pure fecisti. Multotiens es ingratus Deo; multotiens repellis gratiam Dei. Non ita detestaris malum ut deberes; in bono non es ita progressivus ut deberes. Sed tu de omnibus petis veniam et paratus es confiteri et satisfacere si Deus reduxerit tibi aliquid ad memoriam, quidquid illud fuerit?

POENITENS: Ita est, domine. (P. 199)

[You have looked evilly at many persons,
both male and female; you have lusted after
them, you have agitated them, you have
fondled them, you have kissed them. Many
other things have passed from your memory;
many are your hidden sins; many are your
omissions. Even the good deeds that you
have done, you have done less purely. Many
times you are ungrateful to God; many times
you refuse God's grace. You do not detest evil
as you should. But are you prepared to beg
forgiveness for your sins and to confess them
and to make satisfaction if God will return
anything to your memory, whatever it will
be?

PENITENT: It is so, Father.]

Despite the Poenitens's detailed confession and his promises to abstain from wrongdoing in the future, he is reminded by the priest that in the final analysis he is still a
despicable, weak-willed sinner. He must do perpetual
penance for the sins that he has neglected to confess, for
secret sins, and for those he has committed and forgotten.
He must be always aware that these sins exist still to be
confessed and must beg forgiveness should he remember
them. He is reminded that even his good deeds have been
done with a motive less pure and that his progress toward
goodness has been all too slow. He is still a backslider and
a sick man—*infirmans*—who must always be on guard
against his *infirmitas*. After warning the penitent always to
feel sorrow for his sins and to sin no more, the priest
allows him to leave the confessional, divested of his self-
esteem, but with a renewed knowledge of his inadequacy
and weakness.

Admittedly, in the *Liber Poenitentialis*, Robert of Flamborough has not created a sinner possessed of considerable depth or dimension. The Poenitens is largely just
an interlocutor who combines great ignorance with great
contrition. His own speeches are limited; it is the con-

fessor's elaborate questions and examples that succeed in creating the penitent's character, the author's method of permitting one speaker in a dialogue to assume the burden of what we might begin to call the "characterization" of the other. This is a method that will later prove effective in John Gower's *Confessio Amantis.*

Roughly contemporary with the *Liber Poenitentialis* is the *Ancrene Wisse.* This prose work, which survives in fourteen manuscripts, was written by a pious and highly literate cleric. The book is divided into eight parts, one of which has to do with confession. Whereas Robert's work had been intended for the instruction of the sinful cleric, the *Wisse* provides interesting insights into the sins that tempt the female religious. As both a religious *and* a woman, she was expected to be better and worse than a man, and therefore in a different category from the male sinner.

In his description of sin, the author of the *Wisse* explains to the women that, since the pious are more strongly tempted by the devil because of their greater good, they must be more strongly prepared to overcome evil. Subsequently, he discusses the seven deadly sins and their progeny, comparing each of the sins to animals, and then turns to a discussion of the "contraries," whereby a sin can be cured by its opposition. Each sin has its remedy, the author says: "Prude salue is eadmodnesse. Ondes. feolahich luue. Wreaððes. Þolemodnesse. Accidies. Redunge. misliche werkes. gastelich froure. ðisceunges. ouerhohe of eorðliche þinges. festschipes. freo heorte."[8] [Pride's salve is humility; Envy's brotherly love; Wrath's patience; Sloth's reading various works of spiritual comfort; Covetousness, contempt for earthly things; Avarice's a generous heart.]

Robert of Flamborough had advised his priest to ask the penitent after every sin: How many? How much? How often? The author of the *Wisse* carries on this same tradition but divides his questions into six categories, or circumstances, and deals with each in a more thorough and systematic manner. The penitent is asked to give detailed answers to "Who or With whom? Where? When? How? How many? Why?"

The first category deals with the person who has committed the sin and with the other person or persons involved. The anchoress is asked by the priest to reveal this and to say,

> Sire ich am a wummon & schulde bi rihte beo mare scheomeful to habben ispeken as ich spec. oðer idon as ich dude. for þi mí sunne is mare þen of a wepmon. for hit bi com me wurse. Ich am an ancre. A nunne. A wif iweddet. a meiden. a wummon Þ me lefde se wel. a wummon þe habbe ear ibeon ibearnd wið swuch þing. & ahte þe be tere forte beon iwarnet. Sire hit wes wið swuch mon. & nempni þenne. munek. Preost. oðer clearc. & of Þ ordre. a weddet mon. a ladles þing. a wummon as ich am. (P. 163)

> [Sir, I am a woman and should by rights be more shameful than to have spoken as I spoke or to have done as I did. Therefore my sin is more than that of a man's, for it becomes me worse. I am an anchoress, a nun, a wedded wife, a maiden, a woman so well loved, a woman who had earlier been burned with such a thing and should the better have been strongly warned. Sir, it was with such a man (and then name him): a monk, a priest, or clerk, and of that order, a wedded man, an innocent thing, a woman such as I am.]

In this section on person, the priest probes his penitent for specificity. It is not enough for the anchoress merely to say that she has committed a sin with "another person," for the magnitude of the sin increases with the circumstances of the person involved. For example, a sin committed by or involving a person who has made holy vows is double, for it entails the breaking of those vows. Also, the female, as noted, is a greater sinner than the male. In this section, the priest reveals a fact that will become more certain with subsequent probing: a sin is rarely a simple, overt act. It is complicated by both interior and exterior conditions and understood only by analysis.

The second circumstance concerns place. The penitent is asked to tell where the sin occurred, for the particular location can intensify the evil involved:

> Sire þus ich pleide oðer spec ichirche. Eede o Ríng i chir-chȝard. biheold hit oþer wreastlunge. & oðre fol gomenes. spec þus oðer pleide biuoren worltliche men. biuoren recluse in ancre hus. ed oþer þurl þen ich schulde. neh hali þing. Ich custe him þer. hondlede him i swuch stude. oðer me seoluen. I chirche ich þohte þus. biheold him ed te weouede. (P. 163).

> [Sir, thus I played or spoke in church. I danced in the church-yard, watched [dancing] or wrestling and other foolish games. I spoke thus or played before worldly men, or before a recluse in an anchoress's house, or at another window than where I should have been, near a holy thing. I kissed him there; I handled him in such a place, or myself. I thought this way in church. I beheld him at the altar].

In this inquiry, the priest is concerned about the physical circumstances of the sin, and not only with symbolic, but with very *real* space. A sin committed in a holy place, such as a graveyard, is more serious than one that occurs in a more secular location—for example, a tavern. One can sense, even when the writer's concern is only to determine the degree of guilt, that the concept of setting qualifies acts of the will. Literary authors in the fourteenth century will often make use of setting for moral contrast. A character should reflect his holy surroundings, and one normally expects pious behavior when the backdrop is a church, a confessional, or a pilgrimage. Yet here the temptation is frequently greater and one often finds the sinner instead. In addition to her elaboration of place, the an-choress in this section confesses that she has taken pleas-ure in lingering over her evil thoughts, perhaps with the intention of carrying them through.

A third circumstance is time, referring both to the occa-sion of the event and to the interval between the contem-plation and the action. This is of major importance in the judging of a sin. The anchoress admits that she is old

enough to have been wiser in her actions. She is advised
to say to the priest,

> Sire ich hit dude in lenten. i feasten dahes. in hali dahes.
> hwen oþre weren ed chirche. Sire ich wes sone ouercumen. &
> is þe sunne mare þen ȝef ich hefde ibeon akeast wið strengðe.
> & feole swenges. Sire ich wes þe bigínnunge hwi swuch þing
> hefde forðȝong. þurh Þ ich com i swuch stude & i swuch time.
> Ich biþohte me ful wel ear þen ich hit eauer dude. hu uuele hit
> were idon. & dude hit noðeleatere. (Pp. 163–64)

> [Sir, I did it in Lent, during feast days, on holy days, when
> others were in church. Sir, I was soon overcome, and the sin
> is more than if I had been accosted with strength and many
> blows. Sir, I was the impetus for such a thing taking place,
> through my coming to such a place and at such a time. I knew
> full well before I ever did it how evil it was, and I did it
> nevertheless.]

Because it was considered more sinful to do evil on holy
days than on ordinary days, the specific day or season of
the sin was important. However, this section on time is
also concerned with volition to sin and with prior knowledge of the sinful deed. It is made very clear that the
sinner knew right from wrong. But her will, which was
free to choose from among the various alternatives, chose
to do evil. She first reflected on her actions, then went to
the place at the particular time that she knew the sin
would occur. This prior knowledge of evil intensifies the
gravity of her deed. In the section on time, the author
seems at pains to show an interior process taking place in
the anchoress's mind, which helps to make her motivation
more psychologically plausible.

The *Ancrene Wisse* is also concerned with the manner in
which sin is committed, and this constitutes the fourth
circumstance:

> Sire þis sunne ich dude þus & o þisse wise. þus ich leornede
> hit earst. þus ich com earst þrin. þus ich dude hit forðward o
> þus feole wisen. þus fulliche. þus scheomeliche. þus ich sohte
> delit hu ich meast mahte pai en mí lustes brune. (P. 164)

[Sir, this sin I did thus and in this manner. In this way I learned of it first. In this way I first came to it. Thus I did it immediately in many ways, fully and shamefully. In this way I sought delight how I might best satisfy my burning lust.]

This discussion of the manner of sinning, along with the previous section on time, paints a vivid picture of a sinner learning to sin and of sin becoming a habit to be indulged. Her character is developed through the repetition and development of a sinful action. Her first knowledge of the deed tempted her to action; she has now become a habitual sinner.

Number, the fifth circumstance, is also concerned with habitual sin, and the penitent is instructed to be aware of the number of times a sin occurs. The lines in this manuscript that originally discussed number have been lost, but it is possible to reconstruct them from a later manual that resembles this section of the *Wisse* in many respects:

Hou ofte/ þat is to seie/ He þat is confessid schal not knowleche oonly his bare synne: but schewe *and* knowleche hou he fille in þat synne. as to seie. hou ofte he dide þat fleischli synne wiþ such a womman. or where þere were but oon or manye/ Hou ofte he spake debatous wordis *and* dispitous wiþ his neiȝbore. hou ofte he dide such wrongis to his neiȝbore. and so foorþe of oþere synnes/ For hard it is to heele a wounde þat is ofte broken.[9]

Again, the penitent is advised to be aware of repeating sinful actions until they become obsessive. The analogy of the festered wound reminds the penitent that a sinful man is also sick.

In considering the sixth circumstance, or cause, the author of the *Wisse* says:

Cause is hwi þu hit dudest. oðer hulpe oþre þer to. oðer þurh hwet hit bigon. Sire ich hit dude for delit. for uuel luue. for biȝete. for fearlac. for flatrunge. Sire ich hit dude for uuel þah þer ne come nan of. Síre mí lihte ondswere. oðer míne lihte lates tulden him earst up o me. Sire of þis word com oþer. of

þis dede wreaððe & vue le wordes. Sire þe acheisun is þis hwi
þ uuel leasteð ȝet. þus wac wes mín heorte. (P. 164)

[Cause is why you did it, or helped others to do it, or how it
began. Sir, I did it for delight, for evil love, for gain, for fear,
for flattery. Sir, I did it for evil, though no evil came of it. Sir,
my light answer or my light behavior enticed him first to me.
Sir, from this word came another, of this deed came wrath
and evil words. Sir, this is the reason why this evil still remains. My heart was so weak.]

The circumstance of cause is that which enables the
penitent to articulate motive. Quite obviously the anchoress is aware that there may be a variety of motives for
the same sin and that one sin may in fact be a motive for
another. A person may commit the sin of *luxuria* for avaricious reasons, for example, or in order to swell his pride
through flattering words. This section also reveals the
Abelardian concept of the sin of evil intention, for, although the sinful actions of the anchoress did not result in
evil, she is guilty nevertheless. This final circumstance
paints an astute picture of the mental complexity behind
actions that seem on the surface to be straightforward, and
one is advised to take neither his own actions nor those of
another at face value.

In the *Ancrene Wisse*, another dimension is added to the
characterization of the sinner. The Poenitens of the *Liber
Poenitentialis* had been delineated mainly by the questions
and explanations about sin given by the Sacerdos; he himself has little to say. On the other hand, the fictional persona of the anchoress created by the author of the *Wisse*
does all the talking herself, for the sections on the circumstances are actually little self-contained monologues. As
she appears in the script written for her by the author, the
anchoress is more knowledgeable about sin than the
Poenitens. She knows, for example, that a number of external factors affect the gravity of sins, that a sin is greater
if it takes place at a certain time or place or if it is habitual.
She is aware of the roles of will and motive in sinful ac-

tions. Often she has purposely enticed others to share in her evil.

The circumstances reveal the anchoress to be an introspective sinner. Throughout her "confession" she subjects herself to self-evaluation. She knows that she should feel contrition for her wrongdoing, but this is not always easy for her to accomplish. She realizes that secular games are foolish and that she should not take part, but the outside world is enticing. She is conscious that her will is weak, that she is soon overcome, and that the sin she commits so easily is therefore graver. This anchoress sins for various reasons, all of which she can identify. Avaricious and vain, she is especially vulnerable in these areas. Most important, however, are the temptations to lust. With flirtatious talk and actions she entices men to her, and once she is aroused, she quickly succumbs. In church, her wanton thoughts take precedence over her holy ones.

Even in this early work, the confessional has become the agent for the analysis of character and plot. The anchoress is encouraged to understand herself precisely because the author knows the ins and outs of her personality. Not only does he define the character of the anchoress, but he also constructs the sections on the circumstances in such a way that they delineate possible protonarrative scenes. The monologues serve as a scenario for the penitent, giving her words and stage directions. Rather than *probe* her, he creates a part for her to fill. He literally shows her how to become deep.

When the *Ancrene Wisse* and the *Liber Poenitentialis* were being written, penitential doctrine was still esoteric, mostly limited to higher clergy and religious. However, there was a large audience in England made up primarily of laity and lesser clergy who awaited an education on the subject. Whereupon, the bishops issued a number of synodalia, or decrees, which as a whole were "the most practical and conscientious attempt by the ecclesiastical authorities of the time to acquaint a mainly plebeian and ignorant parochial clergy with the rudiments of the Christian faith and the obligations which attached to the cure of souls"[10] Once this information had filtered down to the priests, they could begin to compose sermons intended to explain to their parishioners the various aspects of the penitential doctrine.

In their general outline, the statutes that were issued throughout the century are aimed at enlightening the clergy.[11] Similar in content and form, these documents generally concern the ignorance of clerics and their lapses from virtue, often deploring the too-easy penances which they assigned. There is almost always a discussion of the sacraments, with a greater or lesser degree of elaboration, a section on mandatory sermon subjects, and one on proper confession. Originally, many of the statutes contained penitentials, although most of these pieces have been lost. The seven deadly sins are taken up seriatim, along with their progeny, which are sometimes discussed in elaborate detail.

The first bishop to issue a complete set of diocesan constitutions after the Fourth Lateran Council was Richard le Poore for the diocese of Salisbury in 1219, and again for the diocese of Durham in 1228. By 1240, Richard was considered an authority on the council, and these constitutions were to be a model for nearly every subsequent publication issued by the bishops throughout the reign of Henry III.[12] After a general admonishment of the clergy for neglecting their duties and a definition of the various sacraments, the bishop turns to the subject of confession. For Richard, as indeed for English bishops throughout this century, annual confession was insufficient: *Confessiones ter in anno audiantur; ter in anno communicare laici moneantur, in Pascha, in Nathali, in Pentecoste.*[13] [Confessions are to be heard three times annually; three times during the year, the laity are to be instructed to communicate: at Easter, at Christmas, during Pentecost.] Richard ends by reminding the priests that they are to ask questions in the confessional concerning the circumstances of sin and enumerates a number of major sins that are to be confessed.

In 1237, Bishop Alexander of Stavensby issued a set of statutes similar to, but more elaborate than, those of

Richard le Poore. His treatment of the sins is different from that found in the *Liber Poenitentialis* and the *Ancrene Wisse*, for he examines the physical and psychological effects of each sin on the individual himself and on those around him. For example, in examining the sin of *Gulas*, or Gluttony, which he divides into overeating and drunkenness, he presents a spirited portrait of the drunken man: *Per ebrietatem enim pronus est homo ad omnia genera vitiorum perpetranda. Quid mirum. Potus enim immoderate sumptus, ut dicit sapiens, venenum per omnia menbra diffundit. Tunc enim os maledictione plenum est; veloces pedes eorum ad effundendum sanguinem. Tunc venter estuans de facili spumat in libidinem. Tunc oculi vident extraneos et cor loquitur perversa. . . .*[14] [Through drunkenness man is prone to perpetuate all other kinds of sins. What wonder! Drink taken immoderately pours poison throughout the whole body, as the wise man says. Then indeed the mouth is full of cursing. The feet are quick to the shedding of blood. Then the greatly disturbed belly, easily hungering, foams with violent desire. The eyes see strange things and the heart talks perversely.] Alexander goes on to say that the drunken man often destroys both himself and others, either by drowning or by setting fire to his own home and burning himself and his children.

Rather than dealing with personality in the abstract, the bishop has given his sinner specific physical characteristics, so that it is not difficult to visualize this drunken man with his wild eyes, his distended belly, and his deranged speech. In addition, Alexander describes the sinner in the very act of manipulating the plot by recounting situations that naturally grow out of the character's actions. A drunken man, for instance, is prone to violence: . . . *quod ex ebrietate proveniunt guerre, fames, et pestilente, quia ubi plus regnat ebrietas plus accidunt* (II, I, 220). [. . . from drunkenness comes war, famine, and pestilence, because the more drunkenness rules, the more (misfortunes) occur.] The drunken man has become more than his own worst enemy: he is a sinner whose actions have social consequences. However grotesque, he is vital and alive, at least in comparison with the humble passivity of the perfect penitent.

The statutes of the bishops prepared the *layman* for confession through interrogation inside the confessional itself; hence they differ both from the priest's handbook and from admonitions to anchoresses. But it was becoming recognized that this instruction was not sufficient and that laymen should also be taught through homilies delivered by priests in advance. Consequently, a new order was issued on July 26, 1240, which required that every priest know the Ten Commandments, the seven cardinal sins, and the seven sacraments of the Church. These were to be preached frequently to the people.[15] This mandate would become crucial for the sermon literature of the period and was to contribute in an important way to the spreading of the penitential doctrine.

In 1281, a decree issued by Archbishop John Peckham in his *Lambeth Constitutions* made some important additions. Peckham required that every priest should explain *quater in anno*, four times a year, either by himself, or with the help of another, a series of important doctrines of the Church: the fourteen articles of faith, the Ten Commandments, the two evangelical precepts of charity, the seven deadly sins with their progeny, the seven virtues, and the seven sacraments. Each of these texts should be explained on one or more Mass days. Most important of all, they should be explained *populo vulgariter*—in the vernacular. Realizing at last that the laity could not be expected to understand the doctrine of the Church if they could not comprehend the language in which it was taught, the *Constitutions* made provisions for sermons to be delivered not in Latin or Norman-French, but in English. Four times a year, a number of specific theological precepts would be explained. And as all of these could hardly be contained in a single sermon, it follows that more than four Sundays out of the year would have to be devoted to this instruction. Peckham's *Constitutions* was enormously influential. Through the remainder of the thirteenth century and for several hundred years thereafter, clerical manuals—

Pupilla Oculi, Speculum Christiani, Flos Florum, and *Regimen Animarum,* for example—were based on the archbishop's decrees.[16] The *Constitutions* of Bishop Quival's Synod at Exeter in 1287 states that every priest must have a copy of these decrees, as well as lay instructions in the vernacular, or else be penalized a fine of one mark.[17]

The thirteenth-century sermons in English necessarily reached the laity in a way that the *Liber Poenitentialis,* the *Ancrene Wisse,* and the synodalia of the bishops could not hope to do. Very few of these sermons survive, probably because many were transcribed into Latin for preservation and the original copies lost. Of those which do exist, however, the ones from the Lambeth collections (ca. 1225)[18] provide the most interesting examples of the way in which the penitential doctrine was spread through the literature of this genre and reveal the kinds of things that the congregation was taught and that the poets of the thirteenth century and after could expect their audiences to know.

The subject matter of the *Lambeth Homilies* is largely that of shrift, or confession, and they are concerned with explaining plainly those very issues regarding penance which were then occupying the thirteenth-century scholastic theologians. The sermon for Quadragesima Sunday, the first Sunday in Lent, for example, discusses the importance of making a complete confession: "Leofe breoðre and sustre þah we numen scrift of ane sunne oðre of twa. and þe fulie ane nis þet icweme godalmihti. Ne þe preost þe ne mei scrife bute þu wulle heo alforleten."[19] [Dear brethren and sisters, if we make confession of one or two sins and yet follow one, God Almighty will not be well pleased. The priest may not shrive thee, unless thou wilt entirely forsake thy sins.] The preacher goes on to admonish those persons who repeat sins after confessing them by using a metaphor that would later on find its way into Chaucer's *Parson's Tale:* "And eft þu wult bi-haten god almihtin and þine scrifte þet þu wult forleten þine misdede. and nimest scrift þerof. and ferest þe eft and dest þa ilke sunne þenne hafest þu þes hundes laȝe þe nu speoweð and ef hit fret. and bið muchele. fulre þene he wes earðon"

(p. 25). [And after thou wilt promise God Almighty and thy confessor that thou wilt forsake thy misdeeds, and takest shrift thereof and departest afterward and dost the same sins, then followest thou the habits of the hound that now spews and afterwards eateth its vomit, and becomes much fouler than it erewhile was.] The priest then transforms his doctrine into plot and dialogue. The man who goes to confession with the improper attitude is also rebuked. One must go out of shame for his misdeeds and love for God, not because he is afraid that if he does not go he will be found out by the priest and his fellow man. One must always go to confession willing to make full restitution:

> Bluðeliche þe mon wile gan to scrifte and segge þe preoste þet he haueð ireaueð and istolen. and bluðeliche he wule herkien. þet þe preost him leið on. ah þenne þe preost hine hat aȝefen þa ehte þon monne þet hit er ahte. þet he nulle iheren his þonkes. ah he wile seggen. and foxliche smeþien mid worde. Nabbe ic nawiht þer-of ic hit habbe al ispened. . . . Hit mei ilimpen þet he wile seggen þam preoste. Lauerð nat ic hwer heo baoð þeo men þe ic þene herm to dude. Summe beoð deade and summe on oðer stude. ne ic cume to heom nawiht. (P. 31)

> [Joyfully will the man go to shrift and tell the priest that he hath robbed and stole, and joyfully he will hear (the penance) the priest layeth upon him. But when the priest bids him give back the goods to the man that formerly owned them, no longer will he hear it willingly but he will say and foxily smother with words, "I have nought thereof; I have spent it all". . . . It may happen that he will say to the priest, "Sir, I do not know where the men are whom I have wronged. Some are dead, and others have removed; so that I cannot come across them."]

Such sermons indicate that "the everyday characters and scenes which the preachers sketched with such vivid effect in exemplifying their arguments, sooner or later would lead [the listener] on to behold the absurdities of human life."[20] In these sermons life and literature meet, and the sinner therein—in his anatagonistic stand toward his environment, his struggle to achieve his own ends, his willingness to break all the rules to perpetuate his personal causes—becomes an engaging literary character, designed to engage the audience as well as to instruct.

The penitential literature of the thirteenth century—the manuals, synodalia, and sermons—was designed with a double purpose in mind: to teach man the intricacies of the doctrine of sin, so that he might learn to recognize and avoid evil, and to confess properly and save his soul. In so doing it underscored the individuality of each sinner, for as Colin Morris states, "A sense of individual identity and value is implicit in the belief in a God who has called each man by name, who has sought him as a shepherd seeks his lost sheep. Self awareness and serious concern with inner character is encouraged by the conviction that the believer must lay himself open to God, and be remade by the Holy Spirit."[21] Confession, with its emphasis on "self awareness" and the "inner character," encouraged man to "lay himself open" and thus fostered a "psychology" not unlike our modern-day psychoanalysis. Several aspects of this psychology warrant examination in detail.

The Church's suppression of wrongdoing through penance was accomplished by its insistence on humility as the goal for every Christian. In an article entitled "The Christian in the Age of the Id," John A. Hammes uses Freudian terminology to describe the relationship between the Church and the individual in the Middle Ages, which he designates as "the age of the Super-Ego." Man's awareness, he notes, was spiritual. He was often depicted kneeling, a posture symbolizing humility. The medieval ideal of perfection could only be achieved when "the spiritually illuminated Super-Ego should guide the Ego and both should control the Id.[22] It is not difficult to see that this is what mandatory confession was designed to accomplish. Karen Horney's description of Freud's theory of the Super-Ego parallels the concept of the Church's control over the individual conscience:

The [Super-Ego is] an inner agency of a primarily forbidding character. It is like a secret police department, unerringly detecting any trends of forbidden impulses, particularly of an aggressive kind, and punishing the individual inexorably if any are present. . . . The neurotic need for perfection is thus seen as a consequence of the Super-Ego's tyrannical power. The individual had to attain perfection willy-nilly, in order to comply with the Super-Ego and to avoid punishment.[23]

If, for purposes of analogy, the Church can be seen as the Super-Ego, and sinful human nature as the Id, then the sinner becomes the Ego. This concept of "selfness" or egotism is the deadly sin of pride, and in order for one to "attain perfection" this sense of self has necessarily to be destroyed.

The attitude that the sinful self must be denied is the one revealed throughout the penitential manuals of the thirteenth and fourteenth centuries. By means of seemingly endless questions of a specific and very personal nature, the priest probes and "gropes" his penitent, leaving no stone unturned that might conceal a hidden sin for which penance is due. Thus the bad, antisocial side of the sinner is repressed, but along with it go those qualities of spontaneity and individuality which made him unique. When this uniqueness is gone and he is humble, he is also selfless and uniform. According to Bruce Narramore, selflessness, or low self-esteem—which is a component of humility—is a feeling of inadequacy and weakness that the confession of misdeeds does not alleviate but in fact helps to reinforce and maintain:

While confession . . . may help resolve anxiety over the fear of punishment or rejection coming from violation of specific moral standards, it will do nothing to resolve a deep-seated feeling of self-devaluation over one's felt weaknesses and inadequacy. In fact, confessing one's failures can serve to reinforce neurotic self-debasement and actually perpetuate the experience of guilt.[24]

When time after time one fails to achieve the high standards set for him, but instead invariably falls short, he becomes inadequate, devalued, humbled. For not only does this "ecclesiastical Super-Ego" repress the bad, anti-social side of man, but it also restrains "the most alive factors in a human being, such as spontaneous wishes, spontaneous feelings, individual judgment."[25]

The reformed penitent is interesting to us only in a retrospective way; we are curious about the experiences he has gone through in the past. But the penitent is attractive precisely because he is a learner, engaged in a moral psychodrama—a situation of conversion. Such a character, then, is not merely a one-dimensional personification of evil, for the circumstances of sin lend to his actions a sequence of cause and effect, and to his thinking an awareness of how the dark side of man's nature functions. The answer to the question "with whom was the sin committed?" involves an accomplice, which in turn implies character interaction; the "what" of a sin necessitates the distinction between levels of sinful actions; "when" locates the character in real, as opposed to symbolic, time; "where" provides a distinct historical setting for the sinner and entails a consciousness of surroundings as separate from self; and, finally, the "why" of a sin forces an analysis of thought and no longer limits the self merely to words and deeds. These circumstances delineate first the sinner, and eventually the fictional character, by presenting him to us through a variety of perspectives.

Because the thirteenth-century doctrine of sin was complex and because the thoughts and actions that sinning entailed were diverse, the characters that emerged from the confessional were naturally rich and intricate ones. In the lists of the major sins and their various manifestations were infinite possibilities for a literary author; there was no need for stereotypes. The interrogation of the penitent entailed a psychological minuteness that focused on the individual, not the group. And the very concept of the penitent involved a sense of change and growth from within. All these elements are essential to effective characterization; confession became a reservoir from which poets could draw.

And, finally, the penitential literature of the thirteenth

century effectively laid the groundwork for an English audience's richer receptivity to literary plots detailing the transactions of sin, such as the fabliaux. The anchoress confesses: "I kissed him; I handled him there in such a place. I thought about him in church; I looked upon him at the altar; my light behavior enticed him to me." Or, again, the Sacerdos describes the envious man: malicious, inventing evil, carrying tales, devising vices. The priest in his homily depicts the would-be penitent who comes to confession for the wrong reason—so that he would not be shamed in front of his peers by the priest—or the one who does not plan to make adequate restitution to the one he has wronged. Because their own lives had been complicated by the doctrine of sin, the medieval audience became more closely attuned to such complications in poetry. The listener is drawn into the work "not as an observer who coolly notes the interaction of patterns . . . but as a participant whose mind is the *locus* of that interaction."[26]

The penitential tradition of the thirteenth century is an important heritage of such fourteenth-century poets as William Langland, John Gower, the *Pearl*-poet, and Geoffrey Chaucer—writers who would make use of the principles of confession in creating the inner life of their characters. The following chapters will illustrate just how they assimilated penitential lore and incorporated it into their poems. The result is a variety of multifaceted sinners, each manipulated according to the dictates of the individual poet's art.

Confession as Characterization in the Literature of Fourteenth-Century England

> þou cristen man! for-þi ta kepe,
> And let þi sin noght wit þe slepe,
> Bot als suith als þou þe mai
> Wit scrift þou wasch it al awai.
>
> (*Cursor Mundi*, V, ll. 25854-57)

By the fourteenth century, man was well instructed on how to "wasch awai" sins with shrift. For more than a hundred years, the medieval layman had been exposed to mandatory points of doctrine. He had been instructed to make restitution for his wrongs, to be humble and count himself for nought, and to sorrow over his sins in a prescribed manner. Layman and priest alike were expected to recite the Confiteor "on ynglische" at the beginning of every Mass,[1] and, before approaching his confessor to be shriven, each penitent was told to "ransake his owne concience. and þat þat he fyndeþ vncleene. loke þat he wasche hem awey wiþ terris of conpunccioun."[2] Even the "ʒong enfaunt" was not exempt from such commands. He was charged by the courtesy books that to "schryue þe in general þou schalle lere/ þy Confiteor. and misereatur in fere."[3] And such poems as "A General Confession" proliferated and were popular throughout the fourteenth century:

Swete ihesu crist, to þe,
copable wrecche ich ȝelde me,
of sennes þat ich habbe ydo
yn al my lyue hider-to,
In pride, yn wraþþe, in vyl enuye,
yn glotonye, yn lecherye,
yn sleuþe, lord, yn þy seruyse,
And of þis wordles couetyse.
To ofte ich habbe yn myne lyue
y-senȝed wit my wittes fyue,
Wit eren yhered, wit eȝen syȝt,
Wit senfol speche dey & nyȝt,
Wit cleppinges, wit kessenge also,
Wit hondes yhandled, wit fet ygwo,
Wit herte senfolliche yþoȝt,
Wit al my body euele ywroȝt;
And of al my folye
Mercy, lord, mercy ich crye.[4]

The English Franciscan friars had become masters at moving sinners to repentance with such lyrics as the above. Poems like this one were probably used to help the penitent recall his sins before confessing them to the priest.[5]

Depending on his level of theological learning, the fourteenth-century man or woman could recount a large variety of sins and circumstances. He could usually identify them when they occurred in real-life situations. If he was more deeply learned, he could debate problems of will and motive and understand differing degrees of sinfulness. Anyone who wished further instruction—layman or cleric—had easy access to penitential manuals that explained various points of doctrine,[6] and these books were plentiful. As one contemporary exclaimed in obvious frustration: "Þer beþ so manye bokes & treatees of vyces & vertues & of dyverse doctrynes, þat þis schort lyfe schalle raþer have anende of anye manne, þanne ha maye owþere studye hem or rede hem."[7] It would have been unusual, to say the least, if a subject as popular as penance had escaped the notice of belletristic writers.

But before proceeding to a discussion of the way in which the Ricardian poets used penitential doctrine, we

must take into account some of the twelfth- and thirteenth-century works—including some Continental works—
in which the treatment of penance was of another sort,
where the focus was not the sinner himself, and where the
pentential influence lacked the precise form it was to take
in the years to come. In France, for example, though the
motif of penance is frequently employed by the medieval
poets, it is never a part of the deep structure of the work,
nor is it ever the focus of the plot. Penance generally mani-
fests itself in the form of remorse, with tears indicating the
contrition of the persona. Jean-Charles Payen, in *Le Motif
du repentir dans la littérature française médiévale*, points out
what has been noted before, that, prior to the development of mandatory confession in 1215, the penitent's
relationship to the priest was merely a passive one.[8]
Therefore, we should not expect to find the active participation on the part of the sinner that will characterize the
works of the fourteenth-century English poets.

Certain genres were more suited to penitential elements
than were others. In the lyrics of the troubadours, for
instance, the act of committing a transgression against
one's lover was a familiar theme. A truly great love would
forgive all wrongs, and an ardent lover would suffer un-
told mental anguish in order to gain his beloved. To ap-
pease his capricious lady, the wooer is often obliged to
undertake "penance without sin" or to ask for pardon
without having committed transgression.[9] Payen remarks
that the new theology of Aquinas seemed to have made
the lyric poets more conscience-stricken, more scrupulous
and doubtful of their own merits.[10] The turning away
from the things of this world to those of the next is also a
frequent theme, as the following lyric written by Guillaume IX in the early twelfth century illustrates. But we
should note the vagueness of the diction and the lack of
any precise motive behind the speaker's action:

> De proeza e de joi fui,
> Mais ara partem ambedui,
> Et eu m'irai m'en a scellui
> Ou tut paccador troban fi.

Mout ai estat cuendes e gais,
Mas nostre Seigner nol vos mais;
Ar non puesc plus soffrir lo fais
Tant soi aprochatz de la fi.

Tot ai guerpit cant amar sueill,
Cavaleria et orgueill,
E pos Dieu platz, tot o accueill
E prec li quem reteng am si.

(Sts. VII-VIII-IX)[11]

[I have been a man of valor and joy,
But now I say good-bye to both,
And go away to that One
In whom all sinners can have faith.

I have been courteous and brilliant,
But our Lord wants more;
Now I can no longer suffer the burden;
I am almost near the end.

I have completely given up those things which I loved:
Chivalry and Pride.
And if it pleases God, I accept all things
And pray that He watch over me.]

Here the poet's sorrow is generalized; the burden under which he suffers is never explained, and we do not know just why he is a *paccador*, a sinner. His motive for renouncing chivalry and pride and turning toward God is not even an issue in the poem.

Although one would not normally expect detailed penitential doctrine in a troubadour poem, it might be logical to anticipate such in a twelfth-century passion lyric by Peter Abelard. "Good Friday: The Third Nocturn" expresses the poet's remorse for all the sinful souls for whom Christ died. He laments their *crimina* and reflects on the suffering they experience for their wicked deeds:

Solus ad victimam procedis, Domine,
morti te offerens quam venis tollere:
quid nos miserrimi possumus dicere
qui quae commisimus scimus te luere?

Nostra sunt, Domine, nostra sunt crimina:
quid tua criminum facis supplicia?
quibus sic compati fac nostra pectora,
ut vel compassio digna sit venia.

Nox ista flebilis praesensque triduum
quod demorabitur fletus sit vesperum,
donec laetitiae mane gratissimum
surgente Domino sit maestis redditum.

Tu tibe compati sic fac nos, Domine,
tuae participes ut simus gloriae;
sic praesens triduum in luctu ducere,
ut risum tribuas paschalis gratiae.

[Alone to the sacrifice thou goest, Lord,
Giving thyself to death whom thou hast slain.
For us thy wretched folk is any word,
Who know that for our sins this is thy pain?

For they are ours, O Lord, our deeds, our deeds,
Why must thou suffer torture for our sins?
Let our hearts suffer for thy passion, Lord,
That sheer compassion may thy mercy win.

This is that night of tears, the three days' space,
Sorrow abiding of the eventide,
Until the day break with the risen Christ,
And hearts that sorrowed shall be satisfied.

So may our hearts have pity on thee, Lord,
That they may sharers of thy glory be:
Heavy with weeping may the three days pass,
To win the laughter of thine Easter Day.][12]

The sins mentioned in this poem are grievous enough for
Christ to suffer great torture for them, but the acts themselves—unlike those noted in "A General Confession"
above—remain undefined in a way that the fourteenth
century would consider unsatisfactory. Certainly well-
versed in the contemporary theological issues concerning
penance, Abelard simply chose not to use them in this
poem.

     Unlike the lyrics, the late-twelfth- and early-thirteenth-century romances, both English and French, are rarely used to convey penitential themes, for the protagonists are more concerned with serving their king than their God. The emphasis is on battles, and the heroes are caught up in action, not introspection. Even though the "historic" plot may be one of great tragic consequence, the atmosphere is generally one of gaiety. In the fourteenth-century alliterative *Morte Arthure* and in Malory's *Morte*, Arthur is clearly conceived of as a proud sinner who has shed much blood in unholy wars. He is told to "shrive thee of thy shame and shape for thine end."[13] But in Geoffrey of Monmouth's twelfth-century *Historia Regum Britanniae* and in Laȝamon's *Roman de Brute* (ca. 1205), Arthur's killing and plundering are not a "sin," but rather a part of his heroic role. Laȝamon says of Arthur's men that

> Ælc hafede an heorte:
> leches heȝe
> and litte þat he weore:
> betere þan his were.[14]

Arthur's own anger and his savage treatment of his enemies is described in depth. However, he is never a "sinner" in this heroic literature; rather, he is always the "noblest of kings."

An unusual treatment of character can be found in the late-twelfth-century *Roman de Thèbes*, which does contain elements of penance in the Oedipus story. Upon learning that Laius has ordered the baby Oedipus to be killed, Jocasta deems the king a "sinner" and wails and beats her breast. When Oedipus later discovers that he has killed his father and married his mother, he laments that both he and Jocasta are damned and plans his retribution for his own sins—he will mutilate his body, put out his eyes, and live forever in a pit, bewailing his actions. Yet, in this pre-council poem, the characters seem unaware of possible absolution by the priest, and, instead of making a valid confession, they remain penitent for the remainder of their lives.

Subtle characterization was not a phenomenon of the twelfth and thirteenth centuries. The language that was to make this possible was not yet in common use outside ecclesiastical discussions of sin. Nowhere is this more evident than in the "conversion" literature, such as the miracle plays and the saint's lives. In these works, characters become "good" in a sudden and miraculous way, generally without any feelings of remorse. The specific penitential vocabulary that was to mark the fourteenth-century English œuvres is conspicuously lacking.

The miraculous conversion scene occurs frequently throughout medieval drama, but in the pre-council plays conversion itself is not the central issue—instead the playwright tends to concentrate on events which occur before and after the redemption. In the twelfth-century Fleury play, *The Conversion of the Blessed Apostle Paul,* there are no words at all that indicate repentance or contrition. Paul's "conversion," in fact, is accomplished through stage directions! After Saul has been struck blind, Ananias appears to him and reproaches him for his past actions. The instructions state: *Tunc surgat Saulus et quasi iam credens, et praedicans alta voce, dicat: Cur, Judaei, non resipiscitis? / Veritati cur contradictis?* [Then let Saul rise, and, as if now believing, and preaching in a loud voice, let him say: "Why, O Jews, do you not recover your senses? / Why do you oppose the truth?"][15] In the *Service for Representing Adam,* a twelfth-century Anglo-Norman play, Adam does lament his sins, but only in the now-familiar general terms:

> Allas! chaitif, tant mal vi unches l'ore,
> Que mes pecchez me sunt coru sore,
> Que jo guerpi le Seignor que hom aüre!
>
> [Alas, woe is me, how evil was that hour
> in which my sins overwhelmed me,
> In which I forsook the Lord whom all adore!][16]

Eve's admission of her sins in the same play is certainly contrite enough, but like Adam's lament, her deeds are characterized by nonspecific diction:

Si jo mesfis, jo en suffre la haschee.
Jo sui copable; par Deu serrai jugee.
Jo sui vers Deu e vers toi mult mesfeite;
Le mien mesfait mult iert longe retraite.
Ma culpe est grant, mes pecchiez me dehaite.
Chaitive sui, de tut bien ai suffraite!

[If I have sinned, I suffer the weight of it.
I am guilty; I will be judged by God.
I have sinned greatly toward God and you;
My sin will long be reviled.
My guilt is great, my sins afflict me.
Wretched me, I have lacked all goodness!][17]

The *Golden Legend* of Jacobus de Voragine was written during the last quarter of the twelfth century, but it contains a number of saints' lives that had been circulating for years, which contain throughout a pattern suggestive of the pre-council literature. The saints, in order to instruct the audience by their extraordinary faith, virtue, and ability to withstand numerous tortures, must confront the heathen during the course of the tale and must somehow convert him. But these "conversion" scenes are lacking in subtlety; the persons converted are never individualized; and they are always of perfunctory importance to the plot, which is concerned solely with the glorification of that saint. In the legend of Saint John Chrysostom, for example, a barbaric Celt named Ganias, who had always "lusted for power," was frightened when an army of angels repulsed his soldiers. Consequently, he "acknowledged his wrongs" and without further ado became "humble and respectful."[18] The emperor Trajan, upon seeing how stoically Saint Ignatius bore his torture by wild beasts, "had remorse for the ills which he had heaped upon Ignatius," and forthwith ceased seeking out Christians to persecute.[19] And Saint Catherine's learned debate with fifty pagan orators on the respective merits of Christian worship produced such instant results that even the saint must have been proud: "Wherefore, O Emperor," the defeated orators exclaimed, "we do constantly confess that, unless thou canst proffer a more probable opinion in favor of the gods whom we have until now adored, we are all converted, and believe in Christ!"[20] Formulaic in plot, these legends are never concerned with the interior processes of sin or with the complicated motives behind a real repentance.

But by the fourteenth century the penitential tradition began to produce characters who were richer and more resonant than those described above. Rather than playing a peripheral part in the action, the sinner became the central focus of the work of art, his interior nature shaped by the penitential manuals and drawn from the mental processes defined by scholastic debate. Such a character came to be dealt with in a singular way and can be subjected to a kind of "penitential analysis."

Certain aspects of the sacrament of penance can be found in the characters of the Ricardian poets— in *Piers Plowman*, the *Confessio Amantis*, the poems of the *Cotton Nero A.x.*, and the *Canterbury Tales*. The protagonists of these poems, and some of the minor characters as well, are distinctly conceived of as sinners—logical outgrowths of the penitential ambience—but to a greater or lesser degree. The insistence on confession to a priest had taken deep root in the medieval mind, for the sinner in the works of these poets never acts alone. Always included is a character, be he priest or layman, who functions as a confessor, and some kind of "confession" takes place, but it is not necessarily a valid one. Much can be revealed about a character who flagrantly violates the rules promulgated by the *Omnis utriusque sexus* decree. A true penitent will undergo a change from egotism to humility and will ultimately learn something in the process, but a false confessant will make no change at all and will discover nothing about himself.

The truly contrite individual will discover his own lack of self-worth, and his self-esteem, which has constituted his personality from the beginning, will be shattered. His grandiose ideas about his own importance in the universe will be replaced by the Christian assertion that man is a lowly, inglorious creature who should sorrow perpetually for his misdeeds rather than strut upon the stage of life. It is not merely chance that most of the sinners are guilty of pride. Like the Poenitens, they must be brought low before any radical character change can take place. So their "confessors" methodically attack each of those attributes the sinners are proudest of and reduce them to nothing. This is the way the penitent acquires self-knowledge. But at this point a poem that has concerned itself with the learning process will come swiftly to an end, or else the reformed penitent will disappear from the work. Because of his newly acquired passivity, he is unable to further the plot and becomes less interesting as a literary character. For this reason, Langland, Gower, the *Pearl*-poet, and Chaucer are not so concerned with the reformed penitent as with the mind of the sinner while he is still a sinner.

A character's diction can be crucial to an understanding of his conversion from sinner to reformed penitent. All of the poems in this chapter contain word clusters that convey certain moral distinctions, inseparable from their generally established meanings. For instance, dialogues that include such words as *absolve, repent, guilt, shame, grope, confess*, and *intent* force the reader to recall penance. Also important are words that denote the circumstances—who? what? where? why? how?—particularly if they are used together or are spoken by a character acting as a priest. On the other hand, important words are often lacking in a context in which they ordinarily belong: words indicating contrition when a "confession" is taking place or intention to make satisfaction when the confession has ended. At other times, the poet gives his audience certain word clues by which to determine a character's internal sinfulness and to fathom a mind delighting over sinful thoughts or motivated by hate. And, finally, in the works of this type, there is often a direct link between the words spoken by a sinful character and the material contained in a penitential manual.

The above method of the English poets contrasts vividly with the scheme employed by Dante in his great treatise on sin, the *Commedia.* Although Dante the pilgrim does pass through an ignorance of sin before Hell, to a knowledge of sin after Hell and a cleansing in Purgatory, his function throughout the poem is largely that of an Everyman. Not shown as an active sinner, he is an observer, a learner, open to all sins, but participating in them only in a symbolic way.[21] Virgil, himself an inhabitant of Purgatory, can officiate only as a tour guide, not as a priest who probes and gropes his penitent to bring about a full confession and subsequent character change. When Dante does "confess" to Beatrice in Book XXXI of the *Purgatorio,* it is strangely wordless:

> Era la mia virtù tanto confusa
> che la voce mosse, e pria si spense
> che dalli organi suoi fosse dischiusa.
>
> [My faculties were so confounded
> that my voice began and was spent
> before it was released from its organs.][22]
>
> Si scoppia' io sott'esso grave carco,
> fuori sgorango lacrime e sospiri,
> e la voce allentò per sou varco.
>
> [So I broke down under that heavy charge,
> pouring forth tears and sighs,
> and my voice failed in its passage.][23]

Never is the *selva oscura,* the "dark wood," mentioned at the beginning of the *Inferno,* examined to see just what secret sins it might contain. Nor is Dante the pilgrim questioned concerning the "entente" and the circumstances of his actions following the method outlined by the penitential manuals of his day. The characters he meets during the course of his journey are in a static state: those in Hell can never repent; those in Purgatory can only repent. Dante's own knowledge of penance permeates his poem, but he did not choose to subject his sinners to that kind of "penitential analysis" peculiar to the English poets of the fourteenth century. An examination of the sinners in *Piers*

Plowman will illustrate the way in which this analysis can be put to use.

William Langland's familiarity with the sacrament of penance is apparent on a first reading of *Piers Plowman.* The poem is, as Morton Bloomfield states, a journey toward salvation and perfection in which penance is a most important step.[24] A number of the Latin quotations in the poem indicate that the poet had read some manual for parish priests.[25] Langland himself was probably an ecclesiast in minor orders,[26] and the work was probably intended to be read by the clergy throughout England.[27] Given this background, one would expect the poet to make conscious and deliberate use of the penitential tradition in the creation of his sinful characters; yet, this aspect of his work has been previously overlooked.

In a recent article, John A. Alford comments on the role of the Latin quotations in *Piers Plowman,* refuting such critics as J. J. Jusserand and, more recently, George Kane, who contend that the poem shows a careless lack of detailed planning.[28] Instead, Alford contends, Langland relies heavily on secondary sources available to him. Alford envisions the poet "eking out his poem slowly, even tediously, while poring over a variety of commentaries and preacher's aids."[29] For at least a part of the time during his composition of the poem, Langland must also have had at his disposal a *liber poenitentialis,* for the direct influence of the penitentials can be seen in the poet's handling of Passus VII and VIII, in the confession of the Seven Deadly Sins to Repentance, who acts as their priest.

On a number of occasions the questions asked by the priest of the penitent in confessional manuals seem to have directly affected Langland's choice of the Sins's speeches. Because these handbooks, as we have seen, are never "original," it is possible to illustrate this influence by the use of John Mirk's *Instructions for Parish Priests.* When the questions from the *Instructions* are placed alongside parallel sections from *Piers Plowman,* the resemblances are remarkably close. In the *Instructions,* the priest asks the

penitent about his sins of Pride, and here Langland's
Superbia is allowed to answer:

MIRK: Hast þow ben inobedyent
            A-gayn goddes cummawndement?
                                        (ll. 979–80)

LANGLAND: For ich formest and ferst . to fader and to
               moder
            Haue ybe vnboxome . ich biseche god of mercy;
            And vnboxome ybe . nouht a-baissed to a-gulte
            God and alle good men . so gret was myn
               herte;
            In-obedient to holy churche . and to hem þat
               þer seruen.
                                        (VII, 15–19)

MIRK: Hast þou any tyme by veyn glory
            I-þoght þy self so holy,
            Þat þow hast had any dedeyn
            Of oþer synfulle þat þou hast seyn?
                                        (ll. 1045–48)

LANGLAND: [I have] scorned hem and oþere . yf
            [ich] a skyle founde.
                                        (VII, 22).

MIRK: Hast þou also prowde I-be
            Of any vertu þat god ȝaf þe?
            For þy voys was gode & hye,
            Or for þy wyt was gode & slye,
            Or for thy herus were cryspe & longe,
            Or for þow hast a renabulle
            [reasonable] tonge,
            [Or for thy body is fayr & long,
            Or for þou art white & strong,]
            Or for þy flesch ys whyte and clene,
            Or any syche degre to say at ene?
                                        (ll. 1003–12)

LANGLAND: Wilnede þat men wende . my werkes were þe
               beste,
            And konnyngest of my craft . clerkes oþer
               oþere,
            And strengest vp-on stede . and styuest vnder
               gurdell,

And louelokest to loken on . and lykyngest a
    bedde;
And lykynge of such a lif . þat no lawe preyseþ,
Prout of my faire fetours . and for ich songe
    shulle.

(VII, 41–46)

MIRK: Hast þou be prowde of worschype or gode,
Or for þow come of grete blode?

(ll. 1015–16)

LANGLAND: [I was proud of] what ich knew and couthe .
[and] what kym ich kam of.

(VII, 58)

The sections on the seven deadly sins in the *Instructions*
contain material not included in *Piers Plowman*, and vice
versa. Manuals of sin differed in particulars, although certain topics tended to recur. But the above similarities are
striking.

Other correspondences can be found throughout the
two works. In the segment on *luxuria*, for example, the
priest in the *Instructions* asks with whom the lechery was
committed and if the deed itself was motivated by any
previous physical actions. He asks if the act was aided by
strength or by "scowre." During his "confession," Langland's Luxuria answers all these questions. He ap-
proached "eche maide þat [he] mette" with the desire to
sin. He kissed her about the mouth and "grope[d]" her,
"Til oure boþers wil was on." At times he used both
strength and sorcery in committing the sin. He has even
tried to persuade her with bawdy tunes. Mirk's priest
asks: "Hast þou hade lykynge for to here/ Songes þat of
lechery were?" (11. 1279–80). Langland's Luxuria volunteers this information in his speech: "[I] sotilede songes .
and sende out olde baudes/ For to wynne to my wil .
wommen with gyle" (VII, 189–90). There is even a section
on the circumstances in both works. The priest in the *Instructions* asks to know exactly when the sin took place, so
that he might determine its gravity:

And whenne hyt was, and what day,
Byd hym to the that he say,

> For on a halyday ȝef he synne,
> Nedely to þe he mote hyt mynne,
> Or any oþer fastynge day,
> Lentun or vygyle, as telle he may;
> For gratter synne for soþe hyt ys
> On suche dayes to do a-mys,
> Myche more wythoute nay,
> Þen on a-noþer werkeday.
>
> (ll. 1487–96).

On the subject of time, Luxuria remarks that he has sinned

> As wel fastyngdaies [as] frydaies . and heye-feste euenes,
> As luf in lente as oute of lente . alle tymes liche—
> Suche werkus with ous . were neuere out of seson—
>
> (ll. 182–84)

It seems apparent, then, that Langland had some penitential manual close at hand while composing this section of his poem; which one, we may never know. But his method of allowing the Sins to present themselves through monologues is very close to that used in the anonymous fourteenth-century manual *The Clensyng of Mannes Soule.* The author of this work, after discussing each of the deadly sins, provides model confessions for his readers, where the various sins reveal certain "personality traits" in common with those of Langland's characters. For example, both sins of Sloth are guilty of not saying their prayers properly. In the *clensyng* Sloth admits that when

> [I should have] þouȝte on my god. and speciali in tyme of meditacions or contemplacions. in tyme of seruise or tyme of preier. or tyme of masse heryng or seiyng/ alle suche tymes and oþere tymes y haue sette my wille *and* occupied my mynde aboute þe world and þe fleische. aboute oþere vanitees and ydilnes whiche was not spedeful or needful in þat tyme raþer þan to sette my mynde on þe goodnesse and werkis of my god or on his bittir passions or on [þe] *ver*tuose lyuyng of his blissid modir and of is oþere seyntis. (P. 82, 11. 4–13)

Langland's Sloth also has a tendency to sleep over his prayers. Like his lazy brother, he would sooner "huyre of harlotrye" (VIII, 22) than think on "Godes pyne and hus passion" (VIII, 20). He often lies with his "lemman in [his] armes,/ Tyle matyns and messe be don" (VIII, 26–27). Both sins prefer secular literature to the reciting of religious verse. Sloth in the *Clensyng* admits that he is lax with the Pater Noster and the "bedis" (p. 84, 11. 7–8) but derives great pleasure from "romauncis *and* fablis and songis *and* carollis of dishoneste and synne *and* nycetees (p. 85, 11. 1–2). Langland's Sloth cannot say "parfytliche [his] pater-noster" (VIII, 10) and "bidde[s]" his "bedis" but "can [recite] rymes of robyn hode . and of Randolf, erl of chestre" (VIII, 11), and he is constantly occupied with "ydel tales."

In both works, Sloth is seen to be careless in his dealing with other people. He is neglectful of another's property, causing

> loss or harm of oþere mennes goodis bi
> myskepyng or mysrulyng/ good or catel meete
> or drinke or oþere þingis. (*Clensyng,* p. 86,
> 11. 8–10)

And Langland's Sloth confesses that

> Yf ich bygge and borwe ouht . bote hit be y-tayled,
> Ich for-ȝete [hit] as ȝerne . and yf
> eny man hit askeþ,
> Sixe sithe oþer seuene . ich for-sake
> hit with oþes;
> Thus haue ich tened trewe men . ten
> hondred tymes.
>
> (VIII, 35–38)

Both Sins are loath to perform any of the cardinal works of mercy. Langland's character has "visited neuere feble man . ne feterid man in prisone" (VIII, 21). His counterpart also disdains to "go to prisons" (p. 90, 1. 80). Further, he admits that he has

> not ȝoue bodili meete to þe hungri/
> ne bodili drinke to hem þat ben þristi .
> whanne y hadde/ to ȝeue hem/ or if y

myȝte not counforte hem: y
hadde/ no compassion of hem . (P. 89, 11. 11–14)

And, finally, both characters show eventual repentance
for all the slothful deeds they have committed. Langland's
Sloth promises that he will attend church regularly, "as ich
a monke were," and will go to evensong as well. Thus, the
tale of these Sins is brought to its close.

In *Piers Plowman*, Langland has revealed his indebted-
ness to the penitential manuals for the creation of the
characters of his Seven Deadly Sins. But there are other
confessions in the poem as well, and the poet puts his
knowledge of the penitential tradition to use in creating
sinners of a different kind. In the "confession" of Lady
Meed, Langland uses the device of the false confession,
coupled with Abelard's concept of subjective intent.

The key to Meed's personality is given early by Theology, who says:

Mede is moillere . amendes was here dame
Þouh fals were hure fader . and fykel-tonge hure syre,
Amendes was hure [moder] . by trewe [mennes] lokyng.
(III, 120–22)

Meed has the potential for either good or evil, but of herself she is neutral. Those who receive her services lend her
morality according to their own intent. As Abelard had
stated two centuries before, *Sepe quippe idem a diuersis
agitur, per iusticiam unius et per nequitiam alterius. . . . [The
same thing is often done by different people, justly by one and
wickedly by another. . . . (Ethics*, p. 26)]. Langland stresses
Meed's ambivalence throughout the poem. It is her
beneficiaries who make her either good or evil: Will, the
narrator, notes that Saint Lawrence the Levite believed
man deserves meed on earth, thus endowing Meed with
positive qualities; but when the lady is shown giving silver
to Simony she is seen to be foul. Her potential husbands,
Conscience and False, emphasize her divided nature, as
does her false confession to the evil friar.

In the phrasing of the confession scene, Langland uses words specifically designed to evoke a negative response from his audience. Having seen Meed give silver to those clerks who interceded in her behalf with the king, the friar is eager for his share. Approaching the lady, he says "myldelich":

> Thauh lered men and lewede . had layen by
> þe boþe
> And falshede yfounden þe . al þis fourty
> wynter,
> Ich shal a-soily þe my-selue . for a seem
> [of] whete,
> And ȝut be þy bedman . and brynge a-doun
> conscience
> A-mong kynges and knyȝtes . and clerkus, if þe lyke.
>
> (IV, 40-44)

Piers Plowman, of course, is not a confessional manual. But, as we have seen earlier, Langland was fully aware of what made up confessional ethics. The priest was expected to extract from the penitent himself a statement of his sin and guilt, not articulate his wrongdoing for him. A priest was not to absolve a penitent who did not feel contrite (and there is no evidence that Meed feels any sorrow), and the confessor was required to probe into the soul of the penitent and was expressly forbidden to administer any of the sacraments for money.[30] The friar's entire character, then, is made up of violations against the penitential code. And when Meed confesses, it is "Shameles, y leyue/ [She] told hym a tale." Having learned nothing from this sham experience, Meed is seen after "confession" bestowing first reward to Peace, then bribery to Men of Law.

A third "confession scene" in *Piers Plowman* involves the flamboyant Hawkyn, or Activa-vita, symbol of the Active Life. With this character, Langland experiments with the "sin-knowledge-humility" formula inherent in the concept of the "penitent." Stella McGuire, though referring to the B-Text, says that the story of Hawkyn "is the story of the passage from self-satisfaction, through the growing awareness of the sinfulness of human nature, to final repentance; and repentance, when it is complete, involves the desire to seek for God and the things that are His.[31] In other words, Hawkyn is to abandon those things which are his own, things in which he has much pride: his music, his ability to make men merry, and his selling of wafers, whereby he feeds the world's hungry. Though the concept of the Active Life was not necessarily a negative one, Langland evidently saw virtue in contemplative withdrawal from the world. Actif is too much involved in life. Therefore, Patience must become his "confessor" and destroy one by one those very aspects of Hawkyn which had made up his personality; eventually, he fades away.

As we might expect, Patience begins by attacking Hawkyn's pride. The minstrel should not feel that he is essential to the world, Patience declares. After all, man does not live by the wafers of Actif, but rather by the word of God. " 'Haue, actyf,' " quaþ pacience . " 'and eet this when þe hungreþ'" (XVI, 252) . Nor must the minstrel cultivate exuberance, but rather restraint: be "sobre . of syght, and of tounge boþe, / In ondyng, in handlyng . in alle þy fyue wittes" (XVI, 256–57). He must have "meeknesse and Mylde speche" (XVI, 277), "alle perilis to suffre" (XVI, 280). "Pouerte and pacience . plese more god almyghty / Than do ryghtful richesse" (XVI, 281–82). If Hawkyn is truly contrite, he will renounce his worldly goods and espouse a life lived in "lowenesse and in pouerte" (XVII, 18).

Throughout this recitation, Hawkyn has remained strangely silent, "sobre of tongue." Having renounced his sins, the flamboyant wafer-seller, bringer of laughter, feeder of the world's hungry, has been replaced by a character who is so meek and mild that he no longer speaks and cannot determine the action of the poem. Langland then turns his attention to Will, the last of the major sinners in *Piers Plowman*.

Long Will, the narrator of *Piers Plowman*, is an individual, Will Langland; but he is also an abstract quality, the human will. As an individual, he is a vague character, described only at the beginning of the poem, where he is dressed "in Abit as an Ermite . *vnholy* of werkes" (I, 3) [emphasis added]. The poem, however, is less concerned with probing the psyche of Long Will than with the education of the human will. In order for the will to choose *bonum in communis*, it must be able to recognize that good. Therefore, Will's most dominant characteristics are those which pertain to his education: his persistent curiosity concerning how man should save his soul, his lack of knowledge about spiritual matters, and his inability to understand what is told to him: " 'ich haue no kynde knowyng,' " quaþ ich . " 'ȝe mote kenne me bettere' " (II, 137): " 'Ich haue no kynde knowyng,' quaþ ich. . . . 'ich shal go lerne bettere' " (XI, 55 and 57). In order to learn the good, the will must be able to discern the "false," and Long Will cannot do this. Though he is constantly exposed to spiritual "teachers," there is little evidence that he learns much from their lectures to him: "kenne me by som craft . to knowe þe false!" Will implores Holy Church (III, 4), and she shows him the episode of Lady Meed. But at the conclusion of this drama, he simply wakes up without comment ("Thus ich a-waked"), and subsequent events indicate that he has not profited from the vision.

This abstract will is never able to understand the good in order to espouse it, and Long Will cannot make a truthful and valid confession. His failure to find Truth, therefore, parallels his failure at Christian renewal. Although several times during the course of the poem he assumes the attitude of a penitent—kneeling before his spiritual teachers, wailing before the cross, even bribing a friar for easy absolution—at the poem's end he is still questing, still unfocused, still unlearned. He "romes" through contrition and confession and watches while a battered and beaten conscience goes off in a frantic search for Piers. Then he simply wakes from his dream back into that world of "trickery, tresoun, and gyle" represented by the folk on the field. Because he never makes a proper confession and subsequent restitution, Will's character cannot develop. Like Lady Meed, he simply ends where he began.[32]

In *Piers Plowman*, Langland has illustrated a number of ways in which the penitential tradition could be used for the creation of fictional characters. In the *Confessio Amantis*, John Gower chose to explore the effects of confession on a single character, that of Amans, and to investigate the relationship that exists between penitent and priest.[33] Therefore, he selected as a framework the confessional itself, based the character of Genius on that of the model confessor,[34] and put Amans in the position of the "learner."

Gower's audience for the *Confessio* was a secular one, which would rather have heard about a contrite penitent who has sinned against love and the courtly code than about one who has sinned against God. Obligingly, the poet combined two traditions and created a courtly penitent who confesses his sins against love to Venus's priest, but who in the end renounces his earthly love, discovers his own lowliness, and turns his attention to God.[35] Such a work must have delighted Gower's audience, who would hear the words of confession used in a novel way. The structure of the poem and the personal nature of the questions asked by Genius would have been familiar items at Richard II's court—and perhaps Aman's repeated evasions as well!

An examination of the structure of the *Confessio Amantis* immediately reveals Gower's debt to the format of the confession.[36] Amans approaches his priest with "devocioun/ And with full gret contricioun."[37] He asks his confessor to shrive him so that "ther schal nothing be left behinde" (I. 227), a request that will take on ironic overtones as the poem progresses. Genius begins by warning his penitent against the sins of the senses, a popular item of the confessional manuals, but discusses only two of the senses, seeing and hearing. Next, he turns immediately to the sin of pride (always the first sin in the manuals) and divides that sin into its now familiar progeny.

When Genius begins to question Amans about his knowledge of, and participation in, the various branches of pride, we see that Amans, like Robert's poenitens, does not understand the sin:

> I wot noght, fader, what ye mene:
> Bot this I wolde you beseche,
> That ye me be som weie teche
> What is to ben an ypocrite;
> And thanne if I be forto wyte,
> I wol beknowen, as it is.
> (I, 11. 588–93)

But when Genius defines the sin, relates a tale on the subject, and then asks Amans once again if he is guilty, we are aware of a difference between his "penitent" and the model penitents seen thus far. Amans disclaims any proud actions: he is beneath his lady, he says, and humble, not proud. He is willing to admit only to one small, venial sin: if his lady tells him to go elsewhere, he will "desobeie." Unlike the worthy Poenitens who was willing to admit to anything, Amans will admit to nothing. Therefore, Genius's job is twofold: he must steer Amans through a complete and valid confession, and—to apply a modern psychological term—he must cure him of his "repression." But as Genius works his way through the various aspects of the sin of pride, Amans keeps up his pretense:

> I wolde, fader, that ye wiste,
> Mi conscience lith noght hiere:
> Yit hadde I nevere such matiere,
> Wherof min herte myhte amende
> . . . .
> Thus nedeth me no repentance.
> (I, 11. 2428–31 and 46)

He is not willing to admit, as does the model penitent of the *Clensyng of Mannes Soule*, that he is

Sumtyme makyng/ booste of vertu þat y hadde. *and* seid þat y hadde vertu. whiche y hadde not and more kunnyng. þan y hadde. (P. 73, 11. 15–17)

But Genius persists and confronts Amans with the sin of pride in dress and speech, which Gower might have drawn from any number of manuals of his day. The penitent in the *Clensyng* admits that

> for pompe and pride I haue be to curiouse in myn owne apparaile *and* in oþere mennes in vsyng more ricchesse in aray of cloþing. perri pelour and oþere wise þan my power was. or [my] degre of staat askid/Also in makyng myn arai more semeli more schapli to oþere mennes siȝt" (P. 80, 11. 9–14)

Amans cannot deny this sin, for Genius is not blind, so when Genius asks if he has ever dressed "lich unto the Camelion" (I, 2698), "mor jolif than the brid in Maii" (I, 2703), Amans is forced to confess that he has dressed himself better in hopes to impress his lover. Furthermore, he admits, he takes pride in his carol-singing:

> And also I have ofte assaied
> Rondeal, balade and virelai
> For hire on whom myn herte lai
> To make, and also forto peinte
> Caroles with my wordes qwiente,
> To sette my pourpos alofte.
>
> (I, 2726–31)

The Church warned that such aesthetic activity as this could easily lead one astray; the model penitent in the *Cursor Mundi* also concedes that he "haf hym-self werraod agayn,/ Caroles, iolites, and plaies" (11. 28145–46).

At the end of Book I, Genius has made little headway with his stubborn penitent; nevertheless, he tries to instill in Amans an awareness of pride's contrary, humility. It was the lack of humility that consigned Lucifer to hell, he notes, and cautions Amans to cultivate "humble speche." John Mirk's *Instructions* also contains a section on *Contra superbia,* and here the penitent too is warned to meditate on hell to avoid pride: "þe peynes of helle haue ȝerne in thoȝt, / And domes day for-ȝete thow noght" (11. 1561–62). Genius explains that this is the way one cultivates virtue and humility.

The second book of the *Confessio* concerns the sin of envy, and Gower once again borrows from the penitential manuals to form the questions of Genius and to shape the character of Amans. Genius's first query—"If evere yit thin herte was / Sek of an other mannes hele?" (II, 14–15) and later on, "If thou, my Sone has joie had, / Whan thou an other sihe unglad" (II, 233–34)—is standard in all the contemporary confessional manuals. Amans admits his complicity here but hedges—he is only jealous where his lady is concerned and only with his competition. For when he hears that his competitors

> . . . clymbe upon the whel,
> And whan thei were al schal be wel,
> Thei ben doun throwen ate laste,
> Thanne am I fedd of that thei faste,
> And lawhe of that I se hem loure.
>
> (II 241–45)

Amans is now contrite and vows to follow the advice given to him by his "wys and resonable" priest.

Genius then turns to the branches of envy, first to "detraccioun," or "holding back," which was noted above in chapter 2 with the *Liber Poenitentialis*. Like the Poenitens, Amans too "holds back," "for thogh he preise, he fint som lak" (II, 394). The model penitent in the *Clensyng* admits to "suche enuyous speche or slaunderous speche . . . vsid openli and booldli" (p. 112, 3–4). When he is jealous of his lady's suitors, Amans confesses,

> I sai what evere comth to mowthe,
> And worse I wolde, if that I cowthe;
> For whanne I come unto hir speche,
> Al that I may enquere and seche
> Of such deceipte, I telle it al.
>
> (II, 485–89).

Having articulated this sin, Amans is contrite: "What wol ye, fader, that I do?" (II, 551). Genius responds with the traditional contrary for detraction: "Kep thi tunge stille" (II, 553).[38]

Throughout the remainder of Book II, Genius questions Amans about other envious actions which might have formed a part of this penitent's life: deceit, supplantation, and backbiting—all of which are commonly discussed in penitential manuals as well. After each sin, Amans admits his guilt and implores Genius to absolve his fault. Genius obligingly launches into a discussion of envy's contrary, charity ("Again þis sin es bote to be/ Funden in þe liif of charite," Cursor Mundi, p. 1536, 11. 27724–25), exhorting Amans to lead a merciful life.

The pattern that Gower has established—the discussion of one of the sins, its branches, and, finally, its contrary—continues throughout the Confessio Amantis. Though Amans has sinned against secular love, and though Genius is a priest of Venus, there can be no doubt that the structure and content of the penitential manuals determined to a large extent the form and content of the work. But for the sacrament to be truly efficacious, there must be a change in the character of the penitent, and Gower gives us every indication that he was as familiar with the internal structure of confession as he was with the manuals themselves. Amans changes from an affected, would-be lover, secure in his routinely sinful life, to a man whose sense of self is literally destroyed and replaced by "a deep-seated feeling of self-devaluation over [his own] felt weaknesses and inadequacy."[39]

In the final analysis, it is not Genius who brings about the humiliation of the penitent, though by his questioning he has prepared Amans for it. Throughout the lengthy poem, however, this sinner has demonstrated his stubbornness, and he is clearly not yet ready to

> . . .withdrawe,
> And set [his] herte under that lawe,

> The which of reson is governed
> And noght of will.

> (VIII, 2133–36)

Despite Genius's assertion that Amans will "faile," that he is "unwis," and that his persistence "is a Sinne,/ And Sinne mai no pris deserve," Amans insists on pleading his case to the Goddess of Love herself.

The scornful speech of Venus makes Amans at last aware of his own frailty: love is for the young, she says, and Amans is old.

> For loves lust and lockes hore
> In chambre acorden nevermore,
> And thogh thou feigne a yong corage,
> It scheweth wel be the visage
> That olde grisel is no fole.

> (VIII, 2403–7)

To reinforce her point, Venus gives Amans a mirror so that for the first time he can see himself as he really is:

> [I] sih my colour fade,
> Myn yhen dymme and al unglade,
> Mi chiekes thinne, and al my face
> With Elde I myhte se deface,
> So riveled and so wo besein,
> That ther was nothing full ne plein,
> I syh also myn heres hore.
> Mi will was tho to se nomore
> Outwith, for ther was no plesance.

> (VIII, 2825–33)

At last Aman's will is at rest. No longer is he the gay lothario dressing to please his lady, lying to discredit his enemies, jealously watching his competition, hoping for more attention than he gets. Because he is now humble, he is no longer aggressive or assertive, and he can no longer determine the action of the poem. In place of his old, self-absorbed personality he clutches the rosary beads of Divine Love. With these in hand, he makes his way homeward, and the end of the poem reveals "not a fiery transformed Saul, but a man saying a prayer that has unmistakable and gentle homiletic overtones."[40] Genius has kept his promise: nothing is left behind. Amans's complete confession has indeed rid him of all that sinfulness which had made him unique.

Like John Gower, the *Pearl*-poet is interested in man's progress from a state of self-absorption to one of humility. To this end, the structure of each of the poems in manuscript *Cotton Nero A. x.*—*Pearl, Purity, Patience,* and *Sir Gawain and the Green Knight*—is based in part on the theory of contraries stressed by the penitential manuals: pride must be replaced by its corresponding state. Each of the protagonists is presented as a learner who must be taught to renounce self and direct his will toward the common good. To help him achieve this goal, the poet provides his characters with a "confessor"—God in *Patience,* but laymen in each of the other works. The poet's choice of language in these scenes between "priest" and "penitent" is derived directly from the confessional. Significant words occur in such a way as to alert the audience to the poet's intent.

In *Patience,* Jonah is presented to us from the beginning as a proud character, possessed of a stubborn ego. To tackle this problem of ego, John Mirk begins his *Instructions* by asking of the proud penitent:

> Hast þou any tyme wytyngly,
> I-wrathþad þy god greuowsly?
> Hast þow ben inobedyent
> A-gayn goddes cummawndement?
> Hast þou for pruyde I-set at noght
> Hym þat hath þe gode I-taght?
>
> (ll. 977–82)

To these questions Jonah would answer "yes." When God ordered the prophet to preach to the Ninevites, Jonah was "vnglad." He deliberately and "wyþerly" [rebelliously] chose to do the opposite of God's bidding: "Al . . . wrathed [was] his wyt."[41] He envisions himself in a Ninevite prison, twisted in shackles, his eyes gouged out. Scathingly he thinks of the "gaynlych" [gracious] God who would send him on such a mission and rejects the assignment straightaway: "I aproche hit no nerre" (l. 85). Always self-aware, Jonah can explain to the sailors that his sins have caused the ship to sink: "I haf greued my God and gulty am founden" (l. 210). Yet when he speaks to the heathen Ninevites, Jonah, like Amans and Langland's Superbia, scorns those "typped schrewes" (l. 77, erroneously cited by Anderson as l. 73) and "mansed fendes" (l. 82) for their supposed inferiority to him.

The prophet is not only a proud man, but he is also wrathful. The poet describes him as "janglande for tene" (l. 91), "blusch[ing] ful brode" (l. 117), "waymot [bad-tempered]" (l. 492), "joyles" (l. 433), and angry (l. 411). The hypothetical wrathful penitent in the *Instructions* is also a rebel against God's will. Sometimes he is so angry that his "wyt hath be a-go" (l. 1140). His words are "bytter & schrewede" (l. 1145); he is evil-tempered, lashing out at his neighbors; and he has spent quite some "tyme in malencoly" (l. 1157), cursing that which took away his pleasure. Clearly a confession of sins is in order here.

But it is not until Jonah is in the belly of the whale, which "stank as þe deuel" and which the poet likens to "helle," that Jonah's thoughts turn to repentance. The mighty God-defier who disdained Nineveh has become a "mote in at a munster dor" (l. 268)—a speck of dust in a cathedral—and he humbly enumerates his sins with the hope of instant salvation. "Now prynce, of þy prophete pite þou haue" (l. 282), he pleads. Having asked for mercy, he lists his sins as though he were talking to his own priest: "I be fol and fykel and falce of my hert" (l. 283); "I be gulty of gyle, as gaule of prophetes" (l. 285). And he begs once again for mercy: "Haf now mercy of þy man and his mys-dedes" (l. 287). Then quite satisfied in his own mind that he has made things right with God, he finds a seat in the stomach away from the "glaymande glette" and simply waits for God to take the appropriate measures to free him.

But the *Pearl*-poet, the audience, and—as it turns out—even Jonah himself know that this mock confession is not sufficient for restitution. The prophet has been motivated purely by fear and by his uncomfortable quarters. He has not expressed contrition, nor offered restitution. The "þre dayes and þre nyȝt" that he spends "þenkande on dry-ȝtyn" are, like the offering of Cain, inadequate atonement. According to Aquinas, restitution takes place only when the one who has sinned offers that which the offended one loves equally or better than he detested the offense,[42] and God at this point does not want Jonah's prayers. He wants the prophet to go to Nineveh, and Jonah has pur-posefully neglected to offer that. God's "appropriate mea-sures," then, are to do nothing, and the self-satisfied prophet who has removed himself from the scum of the whale cuts a comic figure.

In order for Jonah to be saved, he must repent properly. His sojourn in the stinking fish has put him in mind of the priest's instructions for ridding oneself both of pride and of anger: "Þe peynes of helle haue ȝerne in thoȝt, / And domes day for-ȝete thow noght" (Mirk, ll. 1561–62). This time Jonah has attained sufficient humility. "I am as low as I can get," he wails: "To last mere of vche a mount, man, am I fallen" (l. 320). He now feels contrition: "Þ'acces of anguych . . . hid in my sawle" (l. 325). And he vows to make suitable restitution:

> Bot I dewoutly awowe, þat verray betȝ halden
> Soberly to do þe sacrafyse when I schal saue worþe,
> And offer þe for my hele a ful hol gyfte,
> And halde goud þat þou me hetes, haf here my trauthe.
> (ll. 333–36)

With the offering of a "ful hol gyfte," Jonah has at last completed the requirements. Instantly the whale coughs him up, and he goes off to do God's will.

But Jonah is not long the reformed penitent. When the

Ninevites repent,[43] the prophet's newly acquired humility is replaced by the old proud anger. He rails at God, who has made him feel foolish, for he sees that the people are not destroyed and feels that his trip has been in vain. Tired of living, he wants to die and shouts: "Now, lorde lach out my lyf, hit lastes to longe" (l. 425). But God ignores this request. And Jonah, pouting, retreats to a hillside, deliberately turning his back to the sun, symbolizing his sinfulness and his apathy toward God. It is then that God creates and destroys the woodbine to drive home the point about humility and mercy, and, like the Vulgate book of Jonah which is the author's source, the poem ends at this point. Because the Middle Ages thought of Jonah as a *reformed* penitent, we are to believe that he has learned his lesson.

By his explicit use of language associated with the sacrament of penance, the *Pearl*-poet develops the character of Jonah and creates a tale not merely of a disobedient prophet, but of a confessing penitent as well. Jonah is an aggressive character whose will is driven by forbidden impulses and who is ever seeking his own good. But God consistently deflates his self-assertive gestures,[44] demanding that he direct his attention to the love that he should feel for the Ninevites. Those qualities which have made Jonah unique (and which also make him an attractive literary character), such as his pouting, his grumbling, and his peevishness, must be removed. They are to be replaced by the attributes of the perfect penitent: meekness, subservience, and humility. Jonah can recognize his weaknesses and can speak of them himself. And the poet, because of his knowledge of, and control over, the liturgical language of penance, can add depth to the prophet's speeches as well as dimension to his character.

In *Purity*, the author tries his hand at a different type of character. King Belshazzar is a hardened impenitent, who never "com to knawlach" and cannot, therefore, feel and express guilt and contrition the way that Jonah could. That the poet intended his audience to judge Belshazzar against the standards of the penitent is clear from his prefatory stanzas on the "pearl of penance." If perfect, a pearl shines brightly without dirt or blemish, and if kept in this condition it will not deteriorate, even in old age. If it is not looked after properly, however, it will become stained, and then one must "wasch hir wyth wourschyp in wyn as ho askes, / Ho by kynde schal be-com clerer þen are."[45] Only penance can make man's soul bright again.

Shortly following these lines, the poet introduces the sinful Belshazzar, whose soul is not bright and who is guilty of "olipraunce," "lust," "lecherye," and "loþelych werkkes." Most of all, however, he is guilty of pride, for "he trawed / Þat nauþer in heuen ne [on] erþe hade [he] no pere" (l. 1335–36). Not content that his wickedness be confined to his own locale, he determines that "all þe worlde wyt his wykked dedes" (l. 1360) and begins preparations for a mighty feast.

It is at this banquet that the king is given his chance to repent. God writes him a message on the wall, and Belshazzar calls on Daniel to act as his interpreter. But first Daniel, the lay priest, confronts the king with his sins: "[Thou] hatʒ hofen þy hert agaynes þe hyʒe dryʒt[y]n, / Wyth bobaunce & with blasfamye bost at hym kest" (ll. 1711–12). He relates a lengthy tale of Nebuchadnezzar, the perfect penitent. But still Belshazzar does not heed the warning, even when he hears the meaning of God's words; he continues feasting as before: "Þe solace of þe solempneté in þat sale dured / Of þat farand fest, tyl fayled þe sunne" (ll. 1757–55).

Because the king has hardened his heart, he never understands the lesson of repentance that God and Daniel have tried to teach him. Because he has no knowledge of or sorrow for his sinful deeds, he cannot be taught humility. The penitential motifs in this poem ring like a tolling bell to which Belshazzar never harkens. He dies that night, and his enemies lay waste his lands. At the end of the poem, the poet comments significantly: "Þat watʒ so doʒty þat day & drank of þe vessayl, / Now is a dogge al so dere þat in a dych lygges" (ll. 1791–92). From a king on a throne in life to a dog in a ditch in death—Belshazzar has sunk as low as he can go.

In his characterization of King Belshazzar, the *Pearl*-poet has given us a sinner guilty of pride; an interpreter of sins; a character who is brought low. However, because the protagonist is unrepentant, he cannot change his character in life; his personality cannot develop, and there is no tension within him. He becomes a caricature. As a literary personage, Belshazzar is not totally successful. This was an experiment that the poet would not repeat.

Unlike Belshazzar, the dreamer of *Pearl* is no mortal sinner, but he too is guilty of one of pride's descendants, presumption. His selfish strivings must be subdued, and his will must become one with the will of God. Early in the poem the protagonist, whose "wylle" is "wreched," sits in his garden plot, wallowing in pity at the loss of his Pearl. He complains that she is "spenned" in the dark and wants her returned to him. Immediately he is transported through a dream to heaven, where the Pearl maiden will become his lay confessor, and through a series of specifically designed questions and answers she will teach him humility.

Upon recognizing the maiden in heaven, the dreamer makes his first mistake. He egotistically refers to her as "*my* perle" and begins to speak of the pain he has suffered since she was stolen from him. He concludes with glee:

> I trawed my perle don out of daweȝ.
> Now haf I fonde hyt, I schal ma feste,
> And wony wyth hyt in schyr wod-schaweȝ.[46]

But the maiden sees him as he is: a man who rails against Christ for taking his loved one, who indulges himself in pity, and who denies immortality because it is not something he can see. Assuming the role of confessor, she identifies his sin as pride:

> . . . þat is a poynt o sorquydryȝe,

> Þat vche god mon may euel byseme.
>
> (ll. 309–10)

Then she explains *how* he has gone wrong:

> [By believing] no tale be true to tryȝe
> Bot þat hys one skyl may dem.
>
> (ll. 311–12)

Furthermore, it is presumptuous for the dreamer to think that she is his, for she now belongs to Christ. Against his supposition that he will live with her, she answers disparagingly: "Me þynk þe burde fyrst aske leue" (l. 316). He has noticeably failed to secure God's permission to move in.

The dreamer then tries another tack: he will play on the maiden's pity by reiterating his grief. But instead he occasions her rebuke, for he has revealed yet another fault: melancholia, a branch of ire. And she responds sharply: "Anger gayneȝ þe not a cresse / . . . be not so þro" (ll. 343–44). He has been actively defiant, by "braundysch and bray[ing his] braþeȝ breme" (l. 346). She does not want his defiance, but his submission: "Þou moste abyde [endure] þat [God] schal deme" (l. 348). Hearing her words and desiring her approval, the dreamer tries to explain the motives behind his wrath:

> Ne worþe no wrathþe vnto my Lorde,
> If rapely I raue, spornande in spelle.
> My herte watȝ al wyth mysse remorde,
> As wallande water gotȝ out of welle.
>
> (ll. 362–64)

Now that he has understood something about pride and anger, the dreamer can turn from the subject of his own sin and can question the maiden about her life in heaven and about the sinful state of earth. She tells him that the longer one lives, the more he is exposed to sin. The righteous man ought particularly to avoid taking his "lyf in vayne" (l. 687), "ne glauereȝ her nieȝbor wyth no gyle"

(l. 688). The maiden is literally preaching here, and the dreamer's attitude begins to change. His anger and his cries are tempered, and he can express the kind of humility that leads him to compare his lowly state with her lofty one: "I am bot mokke and mul among," he says to her; "I be bustwys as a blose" (ll. 905 and 911). Jonah became a mote in a whale's maw; Belshazzar, a dog in a ditch. And the dreamer, who had dared to oppose God's will, has become as filth and dust.

But his own stubborn will is not fully subdued. When he is allowed to see the New Jerusalem, he makes one last assertive gesture, one final attempt to attain the forbidden. His human mind gives way to frenzy ("My maneʒ mynde to maddyng malte" [l. 1154]), and he tries to leap across the chasm that separates him from his Pearl. Eager and impetuous—"rasch and ronk"—he is once again guilty of presumption, and, as punishment, he witnesses his final humiliation. No longer is he fit to be even a bystander in heaven. He is instantly awakened from his dream and finds himself brought down to the same garden plot from which it all began.

But all is not the same. His experience has taught him a lesson about pride, and, unlike Jonah and Belshazzar, he is now able to articulate this with a great deal of incisiveness:

> To þat Prynceʒ paye hade I ay bente,
> And ʒerned no more þen watʒ me gyuen,
> And halden me þer in trwe entent,
> As þe perle me prayed þat watʒ so þryuen,
> As helde, drawen to Goddeʒ present,
> To mo of his mysterys I hade ben dryuen.
>
> (ll. 1189–94)

This is the lesson that all penitents must learn and that all confessors—even lay ones—must teach: man must humbly submit to God. Those aggressive strivings must be quelled. The dreamer must be "halden"—restrained, subdued. When he withdraws into himself, he will gain more knowledge of God's mysteries, but he will lose the most

vital and individual factors within himself: his spontaneity, which motivated him to leap that chasm; his
egocentrism, which caused him to manipulate others to
gain his own ends; and his active and defiant show of
grief. The narrator looks back at his old self-absorbed personality and is now appalled by what he sees: "Lorde,
mad hit arn þat agayn þe stryuen,/ Oþer proferen þe oȝt
agayn þy paye" (ll. 1199–1200). And he attempts restitution: the Pearl maiden, whom he had earlier claimed in his
selfishness, he now relinquishes in his selflessness and
commits to God: "And syþen to God I hit bytaȝte/ In
Krysteȝ dere blessyng and myn" (ll. 1207–8). What is left
for the dreamer is the earthly pearl of penance and the
Eucharist, "in þe forme of bred and wyn/ Pe preste vus
scheweȝ vch a daye" (ll. 1209–10) in order that he might
himself someday be without spot and attain his heavenly
Pearl.

   The character of the dreamer has acquired depth and
poignancy through the use of the vocabulary and the emotional attitudes inherited by the poet from the penitential
tradition. His sorrow and anger at having lost his Pearl
become contrition at having offended God; his pride at
having possession of the maiden is replaced by a humble
understanding of his sinfulness and an attempt at restitution. And ultimately the knowledge that he gains through
the catechetical process has given him an insight into life
and death, and he has developed an awareness of his
inner being.

   The penitential motifs in *Sir Gawain and the Green Knight*
are much more overt than those of *Patience, Purity,* and
Pearl, and the knight who goes to confession and fails to
confess the girdle illicitly taken from his host's wife has
occasioned much critical commentary.[47] Gawain's
pentangle, with its penitential doctrine, further associates
the knight with this sacrament,[48] and a provocative reading of the poem offered by John Burrow suggests that
"penitential thinking" actually accounts for much of the
"realism" found in the work.[49] But the extent to which the
Pearl-poet models Gawain and his host on the traditional

roles for penitent and priest as we have seen them developed thus far has not been properly assessed. Like Amans, Jonah, the Dreamer, and the crude model penitent in the *Liber Poenitentialis,* Gawain too is a learner whose pride in self must ultimately give way to humility. And like all medieval priests, Bertilac, the lay confessor, must ask those questions and evoke those inner feelings which can bring about this change.

Gawain's pride, his surquidery, is a major motif of the poem. This becomes clear when the Green Knight (who later turns out to be the "priest" of the Green Chapel) enters Arthur's court and accuses the knights of wrath, hatred, and boasting and then challenges them to live up to their egotistical concepts of themselves by exchanging blows with him: "Where is now your sourquydrye and your conquestes,/ Your gryndellayk [ferocity] and your greme, and your grete wordes?"[50] he demands. Immediately, Gawain accepts the challenge: "I am þe wakkest [of the knights], I wot, and of wyt feblest,/ and lest lur of my lyf, quo laytes þe soþe—" (ll. 354–55).

But here a problem emerges. If Gawain is already self-effacing when the poem begins, then he has nothing to learn about humility. However, the poet takes great pains to indicate that this is not humility and that it is, in fact, false pride. Like the penitents in the confessional manuals, Gawain "pretends to have virtue when he does not," and this speech of his will provide a marked contrast with the end of the poem. Gawain is well aware of his prowess, as subsequent events will illustrate. He should never have accepted such a foolish challenge, the poet laments as the knight rides away, but his "angardez pryde" (l. 681) leads him astray.

Gawain's pride in his own perfection is reflected in the comparison of the knight to the pentangle that he is to wear to meet his challenge:

> Forþy hit acordez to þis knyȝt and to his cler armez
> For ay faythful in fyue and sere fyue syþez

> Gawan watz for gode knawen, and as golde pured,
> Voyded of vche vylany, wyth vertuez ennourned
>   in mote.

(ll. 631–35)

One who knows good and is freed from "vylany"—a word that means "evil" as well as "discourteousness"—is the penitent *after* confession. And the knight who prances away on Gringolet, despite his assiduous attendance at Mass, is not yet truly "shriven."

Gawain's self-esteem is reinforced a number of times throughout the work. The court of Bertilac is well aware of his reputation and is profuse in its praise. Upon his arrival at the castle, the folks "kneled doun on her knes" (l. 818) even before the knight had introduced himself, for he was "worþy hom þoȝt" (l. 819). And the speeches of the lady of the manor in the knight's bedroom on the three days following are saturated with her adulation for his reputation as a lover. With this build-up, it is small wonder that Gawain values his life and that, as the time comes closer for him to lose it, he does not hesitate to accept the green girdle to save himself.

Gawain's confession to the priest immediately after he has taken the girdle and hidden it away is a false one. Aware of the clandestine nature of the gift, the narrator is decidedly tongue-in-cheek when he remarks that

> [Gawain] preuély aproched to a prest, and prayed hym þere
> Þat he wolde lyste his lyf and lern hym better
> How his sawle schulde be saued when he schuld seye
>   heþen.
> Þere he schrof hym schyrly and schewed his mysdedez,
> Of þe more and þe mynne, and merci besechez,
> And of absolucioun he on þe segge calles;
> And he asoyled hym surely and sette hym so clene
> As domezday schulde haf ben diȝt on þe morn.

(ll. 1877–84)

The *Pearl*-poet's audience, having themselves had intensive instruction in the *artes confessorum*, could not have

failed to notice that in Gawain's "clean" confession, which
laid bare his "mysdedez," two elements of the sacrament
are conspicuously absent. Like Jonah's first "confession"
in the whale, there is no mention of shame or contrition
and no attempt to make restitution, and the knight's pious
and unnecessary recitation of venial sins is not an acceptable substitute.

But a true confession is soon to come. At the Green
Chapel, Gawain, wearing the lace, is humiliated by the
Green Knight, who reveals the elaborate apparatus of the
joke that has been played on him. Gawain failed because
he had too much ego. Put simply: he "lufed [his] lyf."
Only now does he react with great emotion: "Alle þe blode
of his brest blende in his face, / þat al he schrank for
schome. / þat þe schalk talked" (ll. 2371–72). The Gawain
who shrinks for shame is a long way from the knight who
accepted the initial challenge with "angardez pryde."

Like all the penitents discussed thus far, Gawain too has
become a learner, and, like the others, he is able to articulate his wrongdoing to his "priest":

> "Corsed worth cowarddyse and couetyse boþe!
> In yow is vylany and vyse þat vertue disstryez."
> Þenne he kaȝt to þe knot, and þe kest lawsez,
> Brayde broþely þe belt to þe burne seluen:
> "Lo! þer þe falssyng, foule mot hit falle!
> For care of þy knokke cowardyse me taȝt
> To acorde me with couetyse, my kynde to forsake,
> Þat is larges and lewté longez to knyȝtez.
> Now am I fawty and falce, and ferde haf ben euer
> Of trecherye and vntrawþe: boþe bityde sorȝe and care!"
> (ll. 2374–84)

Admitting that he possesses all those vices odious to a
knight—cowardice, covetousness, villainy, treachery, and
a lack of integrity—Gawain has attained humility at last. It
is only right that he should be absolved by another knight
and that penance should be assigned to him; indeed, a
medieval audience would expect absolution after a sincere
recitation of sins. The Green Knight complies, saying:

"Þou art confessed so clene beknowen of þy mysses,
And hatz þe penaunce apert of þe poynt of myn egge,
I halde þe polysed of þat plyȝt, and pured as clene
As þou hadez neuer forfeted syþen þou watȝ fyrst borne."

(ll. 2391–94)

The knight has already done "penance" at the end of the axe, but he is instructed by the Green Knight always to wear the lace and to think of the lesson he has learned at the Green Chapel. Gawain agrees that he will wear it "in syngne of [his] surfet," adding: " 'And þus, quen pryde schal me pryk for prowes of armes, / Þe loke to þis luf-lace schal leþe my hert' " (ll. 2437–38). Like all wise and just "confessors," Bertilac has not assigned his penitent more penance than he can bear. (But then, too, Gawain is armed with his sword, and one is reminded of the fate of the too-strict priest in chapter 2!)

Bertilac is not a real priest, and his "absolution" is not binding in a strict theological sense. But it is important that the change in Sir Gawain is brought about precisely through the interaction of characters in this scene. However secular it may be in the final analysis, the dialogue and action here were literally created by the penitential tradition. The poet has chosen the most believable way possible to portray Gawain progressing from pride to "schoeme," to his final self-knowledge and humility, and to endow Bertilac with the wisdom and power to bring this change about. It is for this reason that the poet chose his words with such precision. The scene at the Green Chapel must have had a powerful effect on the *Pearl*-poet's fourteenth-century audience, who were not accustomed to seeing a strictly secular character treated this way.

Gawain does the penance of the Green Knight, but the story is not yet at an end. There is, after all, a social code with which to contend, and Gawain must do one last "penance," undergo one last humiliation at the hands of Arthur's court.[51] Shamefacedly, he tells his epic of iniquity and waits for a reply. But the court is neither scandalized nor awed with his story of sin and shame. Intrigued by the baldric, they choose to wear one, too. Thus, outwardly Gawain is reunited with his peers, but, at the same time, he is separated from them. Because of his experience as a penitent, he has become an initiate. But the lords and ladies who are still involved in their game and who "laȝen loude þerat" (l. 2514) have learned nothing at all.

In each of his four poems, the *Pearl*-poet has broadened the scope of the penitential tradition and has explored various ways in which it might be used in fiction. He has freed his sinners not only from the confessional *per se*, but also from the undisguised figure of the priest, and he has employed the elements of the sacrament of penance—contrition, confession, and satisfaction—in building his story line. Because of his knowledge of the language associated with confession, he is able to use penance as character analysis; to examine will, motive, contrition, and the various degrees of sinfulness; and to analyze man from the hardened sinner to the merely erring human being.

4

Penitential Irony: A Look at Chaucer's Prologues

The very elaboration [of the penitential religion in the Middle Ages] makes the system it represents a likely target for Chaucerian irony. Other vested systems of medieval jargon and behavior—courtly love, chivalry, rhetoric, even allegorical exegesis—are treated with less than a perfect reverence. . . . Thus we might predict, *a priori,* that the system of penance, like all worldly systems, would have no special privileges and that Chaucer would not suddenly change his tone and speak with a perfectly straight face.[1]

The most memorable of the characters in Chaucer's *Canterbury Tales* are without doubt the sinners: the golden-thumbed Miller, the drunken Cook, the wanton Friar. Even the Prioress, hardly a mortal sinner by anyone's standards, is remembered more for her misplaced piety than for any good qualities that she might possess. Indeed, the Pilgrims, the pilgrimage framework, The Parson's Tale on penance, and Chaucer's own literary confession in hopes that he might be saved, seem to be parts of a larger whole, voussoirs of an arch whose design is not yet clear.

Just what Chaucer was trying to say about sins and sinners first became the subject of controversy in 1914, when Frederick Tupper, in "Chaucer and the Seven Deadly Sins," contended that the *Canterbury Tales* contains various "Sins' Stories" in which the seven deadly sins are each exemplified by certain characters and tales: pride, by

The Wife of Bath's Tale; avarice and gluttony, by the Pardoner's; envy, by the Man of Law's; idleness, by the Second Nun's; wrath, by the Manciple's; and lechery, by the Physician's. Tupper further noted that each story is accompanied by preaching against either the sin in question or its progeny. The Parson's Tale, which discusses all of the sins, reflects various aspects of each "Sin's Tale." The Parson's examination of pride, for example, contains motifs that would later be found in the character of the Wife of Bath; his discussion of avarice and gluttony, in the character of the Pardoner.[2]

Tupper's theory is an interesting one, but as John Livingston Lowes was quick to point out, Chaucer's scheme is not so pat. By means of extensive listing of the sins and their offspring, Lowes illustrates that there are no rigid categories as Tupper had assumed but that these offspring actually overlap. For instance, various penitential manuals list "discord" as a branch of pride, wrath, envy, avarice, and gluttony. Lying is associated with all the deadly sins at one time or another, except that of envy.[3]

While Tupper had tried to show that each "Sin's Story" illustrated one sin and one only, Lowes pointed out that it was indeed possible for a single tale to embody a wide range of sins and progeny. To illustrate, Lowes found in The Pardoner's Tale explicit references to five of the deadly sins (avarice, gluttony, lechery, wrath, and pride), three branches of pride (flattery, hypocrisy, and vainglory), and two of wrath (hate and homicide). In addition, both blasphemy and hazardry are given separate space.[4] Tupper had tried to reduce the number of sins in this tale to two. And, finally, Lowes noted what should have been obvious: the categories of sins are practically all-inclusive. One must necessarily encounter them in any tale involving sin.[5] After arousing a brief interest, Tupper's thesis, that the seven deadly sins are a controlling principle for the *Canterbury Tales,* declined.

It was sixty years before another theory emerged, postulating one vice as the controlling theme of the *Tales.*

Christian K. Zacher, in *Curiosity and Pilgrimage,* claims that the impetus behind the poem is the sin of *curiositas.* He sees two contrary impulses in late English medieval life: "the itch to explore (a vice then called *curiositas*) and the sanctioned practice of pilgrimage."[6] For Zacher, the *Canterbury Tales* embodies a tension. The norms of the devout pilgrimage are present, but the pilgrims are *curiosi.* As a result they pry, tell tales about one another, backbite, break bonds, and quarrel incessantly. This kind of behavior is what *curiositas* led one into.[7] Zacher's study is a provocative one, but it concentrates almost exclusively on the tales, as Tupper's thesis had done. Thus, it largely ignores the pilgrims themselves where they present themselves most vividly—in their own prologues—and it overlooks, as Tupper had also done, Chaucer's debt to the penitential tradition.

Unlike Langland, Gower, and the *Pearl*-poet, whose familiarity with penitential manuals must be inferred through a close textual reading of their works, Chaucer's obvious firsthand knowledge is reflected in The Parson's Tale, a treatise that he either wrote himself or, most likely, adapted from existing manuals, though his exact source has not been found.[8] And unlike his contemporaries who tended to be more somber in their use of the sacrament, Chaucer does not restrain his inevitable humor and adds to the penitential tradition a dimension of irony that his fellow poets had lacked. In the *Canterbury Tales,* Chaucer is writing for a double audience: one which is not aware of his humorous stance and another which understands.

It is no mere accident that the poet chose the pilgrimage framework to serve as a moral touchstone for his poem and to alert his worldly-wise audience at the court of Richard II of more penitential motifs to come. The pilgrimage had been a favorite form of satisfaction for sin since the sixth century. Throughout the years, it gained steadily in popularity, and in the fourteenth century, when traveling conditions had greatly improved, it reached a zenith. There can be little doubt that many of Chaucer's audience had undertaken such a journey themselves. A "Jubilee

Indulgence" held at the shrine of Thomas à Becket in 1370 seems to have brought the poet himself on pilgrimage to Canterbury[9] and perhaps many of the noblemen and noblewomen as well. The detection of Chaucer's penitential motifs might have been a source of courtly amusement—a sophisticated *game,* or diversion. It is now necessary to examine this game and to determine Chaucer's debt to the penitential tradition.

If Chaucer gathers several identifiable sinners together in the context of a pilgrimage, it is logical to ask whether he has appointed a confessor for them. The *Canterbury Tales* contains a number of confessors: the Parson, the "preestes thre" who accompany the Prioress, and the lascivious Friar. Yet the Friar assumes this role (albeit somewhat dubiously) only in his description of himself in the General Prologue: "For he hadde power of confessioun,/ As seyde hymself, moore than a curat" (I [A], 218–19). The "preestes thre," with the exception of the Nun's Priest, do not even materialize and were probably an uncorrected oversight. The Parson, despite his idealized portrait and his discussion of penance at the end of the poem, is never assigned the role of confessor *per se* within the *Canterbury Tales.* Yet there is a character to whom this assignment is given and who in many ways is the most unlikely candidate of the lot. He is the one character whose presence (in addition to Chaucer's) is felt throughout the poem—the owner of the Tabard Inn, Harry Bailly.

Beginning with his first appearance at the end of the General Prologue and continuing through his comments to the pilgrims in the prologues to their tales and in the links between, a particular type of imagery is associated with the innkeeper. Rodney Delasanta, in "The Theme of Judgment in *The Canterbury Tales,*" sees the Host as a "judge, preparing the pilgrims for their final reckoning." They in turn unanimously consent to his offer in the General Prologue to rule over them for the duration of the journey. The word *judgment,* in fact, becomes a keynote of the end of the poem and will sound again and again when the Parson tells his tale: "In one sense the tales . . . [serve] as a prelude to the judgment of the Host, but in another sense the tales, by being inadvertently confessional, will serve as a prelude to the absolution of the Parson and to the greater Judgment beyond for which the pilgrimage is itself preparation."[10]   It is true that the Host serves as a judge of sorts—the tales are told for all the pilgrims to hear,[11] but he alone delivers the verdict; however, a closer examination reveals that his is the type of judgment reserved for the priest. He will serve as an ironic version of a true Father-confessor to these "inadvertently confessional" tales. His tavern, like that mentioned in The Pardoner's Tale, might be construed as a "develes temple," where the acolytes are "develes officeres" who "kyndle and blowe the fyr of lecherye, / That is annexed unto glotonye" (VI[C] 470 and 480–82). Perhaps even his name symbolizes his function, for the word *Bailly* comes from "bailiff," one who keeps reckonings and serves a lord. Indeed, the pilgrims "maad [their] rekenynges" (I[A] 760) to him directly after their supper at the Tabard Inn. They all agree to his terms concerning the journey, and, on the morning that the pilgrimage is to begin, Chaucer the pilgrim says, "[he] gadrede us togidre alle in a flok" (I[A] 824). The biblical metaphor of the shepherd and his flock is clearly associated with a priest—it is basic to the New Testament and to Wycliffite documents and is found in Chaucer's own description of the Parson. The *Concordance to Chaucer* reveals that the image of the gathering of the flock is used only in this section of the *Tales*.[12] Furthermore, the stories that the tavern-owner has assigned and for which he rewards or punishes are at one point specifically referred to as "penance." When the Host expresses a desire to hear a tale from the Cook, the latter is drunk and is napping on his horse. But in the eyes of the Host this does not exempt him from his duty:

> Is that a cook of Londoun, with meschaunce?
> Do hym come forth, he knoweth his penaunce;

For he shal telle a tale, by my fey,
Although it be nat worth a botel hey.

(IX [H] 11–14)

Here the telling of the tales is clearly linked with the
penitential purpose of the pilgrimage. It is indeed
"penaunce" for a hung-over Cook to perform, and for
some of the less skillful narrators to tell their tales. In the
case of Chaucer's own tales or the Monk's lengthy
tragedy, the stories are often "penaunce" for the listeners
as well!

A closer reading reveals additional parallels between
Chaucer's Host and the medieval confessor. Upon hearing
The Shipman's Tale, Harry swears by "corpus Dominus"—
actually "corpus Domini" (the innkeeper has "mistaken"
his cases)—words that would be said by a priest during
the communion service. Chaucer does not use this oath
again. The Host frequently asks for "doctrine" in a tale
and speaks often of the "devel." The warning that priests
were to beware of women, especially those that "ben
schrewes" in their "speche" (*Instructions*, 1. 59), might well
have been heeded by the henpecked Harry. Of his own
wife, he admits that "of hir tonge a labbyng schrewe is
she" (IV [E] 2428). On the other hand, the Host makes
quite clear his distaste for one function of the priest,
preaching:

"What amounteth al this wit?
What shul we speke alday of hooly writ?
The devel made a reve for to preche,"

(I [A] 3901–3)

he exclaims. And again he admonishes the Clerk:

"precheth nat, as freres doon in Lente,
To make us for oure olde synnes wepe."

(IV [E] 12–13)

It is significant that the Host objects to Lenten sermons,
for it was then that friars preached specifically of penance.

And, finally, though a priest was advised to "spak mekelie & frendlie" unto his penitents, Harry is of "rude speche and boold" (VII, 2808), often shouting abusively at the pilgrims along the way.

Chaucer has provided his Host-priest with a goodly number of confessions to hear. Some of the confessions within the *Canterbury Tales* are probably inadvertent ones. The Wife of Bath's Tale, for example, poignantly reveals her desire for youth and beauty; The Merchant's Tale seems to reveal the story of his own "wyves cursednesse." But other confessions are overt and appear in assorted forms. One critic has stated that

> Chaucer has certainly provided a variety of confessional types. In one, the Wife's, the confession is largely unconscious, since the teller is unaware that her boast ought to be a subject of reluctant admission. The opposite pole occurs in the Pardoner's confession, in which the confessant understands precisely the confessional nature of his remarks, reveling in the sin he reveals. . . . The variety of the confessional device is further extended by the Canon's Yeoman, who confesses to a life misspent, in the full knowledge that it has been a waste; but the remorse grows out of a sense of futility, not an understanding of sin. [13]

Other critics have noted the innovative quality of Chaucer's *confessio*,[14] but the precise nature of his originality and the extent of his debt to the sacrament of penance in the development of his characters have yet to be determined. The most fully developed of his confessions—the Canon's Yeoman's, the Pardoner's, the Wife of Bath's, and Chaucer's own—are surprisingly "sacramental," both in content and in form.

One critic notes that the Canon's Yeoman's Prologue and confession "evidently travesties the doctrine and ritual of auricular confession as one finds them outlined in the contemporary didactic works."[15] It is also the confession in which the Host-priest plays the largest and most clearly defined role. That the Canon's Yeoman deliberately turns to the Host when the Parson is present seems odd to this critic, who finally concludes that since the confession is not completely open and "naked" it is fittingly made to one "whose profession requires him daily to listen to such outpourings with at least apparent sympathy."[16] Yet, given the way Chaucer has defined the Host's ironic role in the General Prologue, Harry Bailly is not an odd choice: he is the only logical one.

The Canon's Yeoman's Prologue consists largely of a series of questions by the Host and answers by the Yeoman. These are not randomly chosen by Chaucer but borrowed (and parodied) from the formulas for questioning penitents, especially regarding the circumstances of sin. In the confession, the Host quizzes the Yeoman about the Canon—the innkeeper is curious—and the Yeoman responds by accusing his master of sin.

It has become obvious how important the circumstances of sin were thought to be, not only in the penitentials, but in secular literature as well. Chaucer also uses the circumstances in The Parson's Tale where, for example, the priest is told to ask *who* committed the sin, whether he were "ordred or unordred, wys or fool, clerk or seculeer" (X [I] 960). Here, the Yeoman rides over to the group and paints a glowing picture of his master to them, which prompts a statement from Harry Bailly: "For certein it wolde seme/ Thy lord were wys" (VIII [G] 594–95)—this is *who* he is, a wise man. And he asks: "I pray thee, tel me than,/ Is he a clerk, or noon? telle *what* he is" (VIII [G] 615–16). The Host appears to commence an interrogation that is a profane and secularized version of the questions the priest in the confessional asks the penitent. The Yeoman responds that his master is greater than a clerk. He is an alchemist, capable of paving the streets of Canterbury with silver and gold. The Host believes not a word of this story, for he sees the "great man's" ragged robe and senses that the Yeoman's admiration is misplaced.

The obvious discrepancy between reputation and reality tantalizes the innkeeper, however, and he is moved to ask another question. This time he is curious to know, "*Why* is thy lord so sluttissh, I the preye" (VIII [G] 636). The question that the Host asks is not the "why" that probes for motive. He is simply intrigued by the Canon's shabby dress. Nevertheless, the Yeoman responds by giving the Canon's motive for his sinful deeds. But such an answer calls for him to talk about a sin of which he is a part. Therefore, he must first extract the pledge of secrecy: "(. . . I wol nat avowe that I seye/ And therfore keepe it secree, I yow preye)" (VIII [G] 642–43). This can be explained simply as the Yeoman's desire to avoid recrimination, but it is interesting that just such a promise of silence is also what all penitents have a right to expect from their priests.

The Yeoman's response to the question about the discrepancy between his master's state and appearance is that the Canon has misused his talents and is guilty of the first of the seven deadly sins, that of pride. He is "to wys," says the servant, and that which is overdone becomes a vice (VIII [G] 644–46):

> Wherfore in that I holde hym lewed and nyce.
> For whan a man hath over-greet a wit,
> Ful oft hym happeth to mysusen it.
> So dooth my lord, and that me greveth soore.
>
> (VIII [G] 647–50)

The Canon's Yeoman, then, sees the pursuit of alchemy as did many people in Chaucer's day, "as the devil's work, not an honest occupation of right reason but a madness grounded on overweening pride."[17] The Canon has become a kind of fiend from whom the Yeoman must free himself.

Fearing that by accusing his master of pride he has said too much, the Yeoman becomes reluctant to go further: "I kan sey yow namoore." This does not satisfy the Host, however, who simply brushes aside the objection. Having established the *who, what,* and *why* of the situation, he is eager to find out *how* and *where:*

> Syn of the konnyng of thy lord thow woost,
> Telle *how* he dooth, I pray thee hertely,

> Syn that he is so crafty and so sly.
> *Where* dwelle ye, if it to telle be?
>
> (VIII [G] 653–56)

According to the dictates of the *Omnis utriusque sexus* decree, the priest was always obliged to find out where—
what parish—the penitent came from; and the Yeoman is
not one of Harry's regular "flock." The man responds that
he and his master live in a questionable neighborhood,
"Lurkynge in hernes and lanes blynde," keeping company
with robbers and thieves. Then he turns to the subject of
how the work of an alchemist is done:

> To muchel folk we doon illusioun,
> And borwe gold, be it a pound or two,
> Or ten, or twelve, or manye sommes mo,
> And make hem wenen, at the leeste weye,
> That of a pound we koude make tweye.
> Yet is it fals. . . .
>
> (VIII [G] 673–78)

So far, the interview between the Host and Yeoman seems
to owe something to the "circumstances" of sin in confessional practice. The Yeoman's last answer also reveals
self-knowledge. His motive for alchemy is greed. To ac-
quire the money necessary for their experiments, he and
the Canon dupe innocent people, even though they themselves know that they cannot find the elusive apothecary's
stone. The Yeoman accepts the responsibility for his actions but also blames the sin on the Canon: "He that me
broghte first unto that game, / Er that he dye, sorwe have
he and shame!" (VIII [G] 708–9). He is following good
penitential doctrine in this, for as Chaucer's Parson states
under the fourth circumstance, "They that eggen or con-
senten to the synne been parteners of the synne, and of
the dampnacioun of the synnere" (X [I] 967). The master is
as guilty as the servant, but that, of course, does not excul-
pate the Yeoman.

Throughout the Yeoman's speech, the Canon has
lurked insidiously in the background. The servant is say-

ing too much for his comfort, and he orders the Yeoman to stop his confession or suffer the consequences:

> Hoold thou thy pees, and spek no wordes mo,
> For if thou do, thou shalt it deere abye.
> Thou sclaundrest me heere in this compaignye
> And eek discoverest that thou sholdest hyde.
>
> (VIII [G] 693–96)

Once again the Host steps in, ordering the Yeoman to "telle on, what so bityde, / Of al his thretyng rekke nat a myte!" (VIII [G] 697–98). On a literal level, Harry Bailly is simply curious to hear more; the Yeoman has come to the most interesting part, and the innkeeper has no intention of having it stop there. In his symbolic role of Father-confessor, however, something altogether different is happening, for it appears that here Chaucer alludes to contemporary folklore concerning the effect of confession on the devil. In Robert Mannyng's poem *Handlyng Synne* is an exemplum entitled "The 4th Grace due to Shrift: it shends the Fiend of Hell." This story advises that, if one wants to be free of the devil, he should go to confession, for then the fiend will be "a-shamed to tempt þe" (1. 12019).

> Sykyr þou be, certeynly,
> þe fende þe fleþ ful hastyly:
> whan þou shryuest þe for hys shame,
> þat ys shenshepe [injury] vnto hys name.
>
> (ll. 12025–28)

During this mock-confession of the Yeoman, the Canon has been represented as a kind of "fiend." It is he who first persuaded the Yeoman to live a sinful life, and he has control of his servant until the latter decides to tell his own sinful story to the Host. When the Canon hears the tale, like the devil in Mannyng's exemplum, "He fledde awey for verray sorwe and shame" (VIII [G] 702), leaving the Yeoman to cry in relief: "The foule feend hym quelle! / For nevere heerafter wol I with hym meete" (VIII [G] 705–6).

Freed from this evil influence, the Yeoman expresses his sorrow and contrition. He now feels ready to abandon his sins and asks for God's help in giving a complete and utterly truthful "confession," as far as he is able:

> . . . for al my smert and al my grief,
> For al my sorwe, labour, and meschief,
> I koude nevere leve it [alchemy] in no wise.
> Now wolde God my wit myghte suffise
> To tellen al that longeth to that art!
> But nathelees yow wol I tellen part.
> Syn that my lord is goon, I wol nat spare,
> Swich thyng as that I knowe, I wol declare.
>
> (VIII [G] 712–19)

By using the device of the confession, Chaucer has created a fast-moving dialogue among three people: the Host, the Yeoman, and the Canon. Behind them one can sense the presence of the priest, the penitent, and the fiend. That is, each character seems indebted to a standard figure in penitential lore, who influences not only the words that a character speaks, but also the relationship that each pilgrim has to the others. The confessional manual seems to have influenced the way Harry Bailly's words evoke guilt, shame, and contrition from the Yeoman. The latter, for his part, prepares for confession in such a way that, like a confessing penitent, he undergoes a change of character in the space of a very few lines. Yet Chaucer has managed this subtly; the characters never for a moment lose their identities or suggest allegorical personages.

The Canon's Yeoman's "confession" comes about largely through the efforts of the Host, who questions the frightened man about the circumstances surrounding his sin. Never does the Yeoman show a real understanding of sin *per se*, however, and his repetition of the phrase "I kan sey yow namoore" indicates that, without the Host to prompt him, he would stop talking entirely. The opposite is true of the Pardoner. Perfectly self-composed throughout his lengthy monologue, he has no need of the services of a "priest." Yet, of all the characters on the Canterbury pilgrimage, it is the Pardoner who is the most hardened sinner. He is, in Robert Miller's phrase, a "scriptural eunuch," guilty of presumption or *peccatum in Spiritum sanctum*, "the one sin which is irremissible, since it involves the refusal of grace."[18] Ironically, he is the pilgrim who is possessed of the most self-knowledge regarding his sinful soul. And he is the most willing and able to articulate this knowledge to the group. Based in part on the open confession of Faux-Semblant in the *Roman de la Rose*,[19] the Pardoner's prologue has been transformed by Chaucer with the help of the subtleties of the language of penance. Thus, this character who usually usurps one function of the priest—pardoning—is now in the role of the self-aware confessant, enumerating his own sins and articulating his own motives.

The priest who has difficulty extracting an admission of sins from the unwilling penitent, according to John Mirk's *Instructions for Parish Priests*, should "grope hym sore"— examine thoroughly his conscience. The Pardoner, however, has no trouble doing his own investigation. Like the priest in the manuals, in his own prologue he lists sin after sin. He first discusses hypocrisy, that branch of pride which he sees as necessary for his trade. All of his relics— the shoulder-bone of the holy Jew's sheep, the horticultural mitten—are worthless rubbish. But they have allowed him to collect "yeer by yeer/ An hundred mark sith [he] was pardoner" (VI [C] 389–90); he is, above all, avaricious. He is an eloquent preacher, as he aptly demonstrates in his tale, but he is also a false one. In his false preaching, the pardoner does precisely what the *Instructions* warns the penitent that he must not. The priest is to ask the confessant,

> Hast þow, for hate or for enuye
> I-holpen or counselet for to lye
> Any mon for to defame,
> Or for to destruye hys gode name?
> Hast þow bacbyted þy neghbore
> For to make hym fare þe worre?

> Hast þow reret any debate
> A-monge þy beʒborus by any hate?
>
> (ll. 1125–32)

The Pardoner's response would be affirmative. For him it is great sport to preach against an enemy. He says:

> For whan I dar noon oother weyes debate,
> Thanne wol I stynge hym with my tonge smerte
> In prechyng, so that he shal nat asterte
> To been defamed falsly, if that he
> Hath trespased to my bretheren or to me.
> For though I telle noght his propre name,
> Men shal wel knowe that it is the same,
> By signes, and by othere circumstances.
> Thus quyte I folk that doon us displesances;
> Thus spitte I out my venym under hewe
> Of hoolynesse, to semen hooly and trewe.
>
> (VI [C] 412–22)

Love is the medicine that "casteth out the venym" from man's heart, says Chaucer's Parson (X [I] 530). But the Pardoner has no love in his soul.

Having thus taken care of his enemies, he will "drynke licour of the vyne, / And have a joly wenche in every toun" (VI [C] 452–53). Despite Chaucer's description of him as a "geldyng" or a "mare," the Pardoner insists that he is a lecher, thus adding another to his growing list of sins.

One purpose of confession, it has become clear, is to make the penitent aware of the motives for his actions. If he can understand the mental processes of sin, he can perhaps do something to change them. Yet, an examination of the Pardoner's prologue reveals not only an obvious understanding of motive and a precise articulation of "entente," but also a contempt for goodness and a determination to continue a sinful life.

Entente is defined by the MED as "purpose, mental or spiritual attitude, reason for doing something" (s.v.). It appears in the Pardoner's prologue four times in sixty lines, and Chaucer is very exact in its use.[20] It indicates not

only this pilgrim's awareness of motive, but also the pride
he takes in himself as a hardened sinner. Behind any good
that he might inadvertently do is his evil intention. The
Pardoner admits that his pulpit eloquence and his preaching against such sins as avarice do turn people away from
that vice. But that is of no consequence to him, for he gives
not a hoot for their souls. He says:

> For myn entente is nat but for to wynne,
> And nothyng for correccioun of synne.
> I rekke nevere, whan that they been beryed,
> Though that hir soules goon a-blakeberyed:
> (VI [C] 403–6)

The Pardoner realizes that many a sermon comes from
"yvel entencioun," but he is determined that the pilgrims
should understand this too. Therefore, he reiterates twice
more in succession:

> . . . myn entente I wol devyse:
> I preche of no thyng but for coveityse
> . . . .
> Yet kan I maken oother folk to twynne
> From avarice, and soore to repente.
> But that is nat my principal entente;
> I preche nothyng but for coveitise.
> (VI [D] 423–24 and 430–34)

One critic remarks that the acts of the Pardoner's typical
audience, as described by this pilgrim during the discussion of his pardons, are a mockery of the sacramental
ritual. Some seek his aid in order that they may continue
their sins. Others, who have "doon synne horrible," must
pretend that they are sinless enough to receive his shrift.
"The Pardoner commits . . . the unpardonable sin of refusing Christ's pardon; yet those who kneel before the Pardoner instead of THE Pardoner, refusing the reality for a
cheap substitute, commit through him that same sin of
denying Christ's pardon."[21] Here again the penitential tradition takes on ironic overtones.

The Pardoner has staged a little confessional drama in which he is the star. He has listed his sins—pride, avarice, anger, lechery, drunkenness, backbiting, hypocrisy—and he has expressed his motives. As one whose profession involves preaching against sins, he understands the implications behind his words; nothing has to be explained to him. He specifically states that he is not contrite. "I rekke never," he says: "I do not care." As a sinner who absolutely refuses to seek grace, he is unpardonable. The fake relics that he carries with him can do him no good. He is one whom the Parson's own penitential manual describes as possessed of "hardnesse of herte in wikkednesse."

Chaucer thus reverses the character traits of the perfect penitent in his creation of the "noble ecclesiaste." He also creates an attitude for this sinner that makes him unique. Nowhere to be found are the humility and the sorrow for sin of the traditional confessant. In the real world, man is not always contrite, and, reflecting this, the Pardoner avows his sins with wit, arrogance, and aplomb. In forming this pilgrim, Chaucer has taken the format of the confessional and has allowed the Pardoner to answer its implied questions in a shockingly impenitent tone of voice. As a character whose ego is always showing, the Pardoner remains psychologically interesting for the duration of the *Canterbury Tales*. He is Chaucer's innovation. None of his contemporaries come close to such a technique.

Even the "epilogue" to the Pardoner's tale is in keeping with the penitential format, but the ending is one that this proud pilgrim did not foresee. In the works studied in the preceding chapter, the self-esteeming sinners are eventually belittled. Each of the characters is made to feel humility by his "confessor" in the area where he is most vulnerable. And the Pardoner, the "gelding" who tries to sell his worthless relics to the Host, is humbled by this "confessor" in the very sensitive area of his sexuality. At the Pardoner's request that the Innkeeper unbuckle his purse and kiss the relics, the Host-priest replies angrily that these objects would not give absolution, but, instead, "Cristes curs."

> I wolde I hadde thy coillons in myn hond
> In stide of relikes or of seintuarie.
> Lat kutte hem of, I wol thee helpe hem carie;
> They shul be shryned in an hogges toord!
>
> (VI [C] 952–55)

The loquacious Pardoner for once is made mute: "[he] answerde nat a word;/ So wrooth he was, no word ne wolde he seye" (VI [C] 956–57). To maintain order, the Knight steps in at this point and demands that the characters forgive one another and that Harry Bailly kiss the Pardoner. He orders that the *pax,* the kiss of peace, take place between the two quarreling pilgrims. Historically, such a gesture was to be given during the Mass by those who wanted charity with their neighbors.[22] Lee Patterson, commenting on the Pardoner's epilogue, notes that it "exactly fulfills the post-confessional part of penance; it provides a satisfaction that fits the sin and a gesture of absolution: 'Anon they kiste, and ryden forth hir weye.' "[23]

In creating the Pardoner, Chaucer has employed the penitential schema but has deviated from the "sin-knowledge-humility" formula of his contemporaries. With the character of the Wife of Bath, he departs once again; the penitential motifs are present, but they are invariably inverted. For "ye shul understonde that in mannes synne is every manere of ordre or ordinaunce turned up-so-doun" (*Par. T.,* X [1] 259). The Wife's theme, submission, is that which is advocated in a religious sense by the Church. But Dame Alisoun's method of attaining submission is decidedly her own.

The Wife begins her story by asking "licence" (permission to confess) from the "worthy Frere." She then launches into a tale of the "scoleiyng" of her first three husbands, all lumped under the category of "goode men, and riche, and olde" (III [D] 197). At first, these men are assertive and aggressive—traits that Alisoun finds displeasing and that she must subdue. Finding her to be sinful, they assume the role of the penitential preacher (Thou "prechest on thy bench," says Alisoun of them collectively) and deliver a sermon that enumerates her sins. To these husbands, she is guilty of "pride," "malencolie," and a lack of chastity. She both covets and chides and hides her other vices as well. By all rights, such a sinner should become humble after acquiring knowledge of her sins; she should beg forgiveness and promise to mend her ways. This is not the case with the Wife, however. Instead, she determines that her *husbands* must become the penitents, submitting to her will.

Taking the pulpit away from these men, she begins to preach about *their* sins, accusing them of lechery, jealousy, drunkenness, wrath, and especially of avarice—for they withhold the keys of their trunks from her. But it is all a lie, for the Wife knows that these man are sinless and that the guilt is in fact her own:

> And al was fals, but that I took witnesse
> On Janekyn, and on my nece also.
> O Lord! the peyne I dide hem and the wo,
> Ful giltelees, by Goddes sweete pyne!
> . . . .
> I koude pleyne, and yit was in the gilt.
>
> (III [D] 382–85 and 387)

Alisoun is relentless in her accusations, and the husbands, who were formerly "priests," admit to sins that they did not commit and become humble "pentitents" instead. Requesting them to take as their example Wilkyn, the "meke" sheep, she instructs them in a mock-priestly fashion on the way they are to act for the remainder of their lives if they hope to receive their reward:

> Ye sholde been al pacient and meke,
> And han a sweete spiced conscience,
> Sith ye so preche of Jobes pacience.
> Suffreth alwey, syn ye so wel kan preche;

And but ye do, certein we shal yow teche
That it is fair to have a wyf in pees.

(III [D] 434–39)

Patience, meekness, and a scrupulous conscience were by no means qualities to be looked for in medieval husbands, but in medieval penitents. On the literal level, total submission will put an end to all this "sinning" and will result in peace about the house. Then Alisoun, like the Host in the Pardoner's prologue, makes a gesture of absolution; she administers her own version of the *pax*; "Com neer, my spouse, lat me ba thy cheke" (III [D] 433). The old men make their "satisfaction" by their generosity (the contrary of their previous avariciousness); they give to their wife "hir lond and hir tresoor." Afterwards, they are "ful *blisful*," a word which in the religious sense means having the "ecstasy of salvation." The Wife's "scoleiyng" process has come to an end, but she continues to govern well, "after [her] lawe." As these old men have "being" only as mouthpieces of antifeminist lore, their story comes to an end once they have been subdued. Alisoun loses interest in talking about them and turns her attention to husbands four and five.

Here the pattern changes. These men, youthful and more virile, take the whip into their own hands. The Wife becomes " in erthe . . . his purgatorie" to her fourth husband, and she eventually conquers the body and soul of Jankyn. But penitential motifs are no longer in evidence. Another treatment of husband as "penitent" would probably have seemed excessive. But the better explanation is probably that the poet abandoned the Wife's prologue at this point. In an article entitled "The Development of the Wife of Bath," R. A. Pratt has argued convincingly that additions were made to the Wife's prologue on several occasions and that the section concerning the fourth and fifth husbands is a later development. He notes that for the earlier section Chaucer had drawn upon the *Aureolus Liber* of Theophrastus, the book that is later read to Alisoun by Jankyn as "The Book of Wikked Wyves." Had the two sections been written at the same time, Chaucer would surely have made mention of the work in the first part. This he does not do. Also, the presence of "oure apprentice Janekyn" in the earlier section suggests that Chaucer had not yet conceived of the other Janekyn, a character developed later.[24] In this last section, then, the poet has simply chosen to travel another route. As he has done in the past, he borrows from the tradition only that which is useful to him in shaping a particular character. When it is no longer appropriate, he is able to let it go.

Chaucer has employed penitential motifs in drawing the character of Alisoun. He has also concerned himself with the subject of her stubborn will. Like the other sinners discussed thus far, she is absorbed in her own personal desires, eschewing entirely the *bonum in communis*. This is especially true in her attitude toward matrimony, which occupies the whole of her prologue. According to Saint Ambrose, for the sacrament of marriage to be efficacious, there must be harmony *(armonia)* in the relationship, and the couple must enter into the union with the full intention of achieving such peace.[25] As we can see, however, Alisoun's motivation is contrary to that advocated by the Church; there will be no *armonia* until her spouses submit to her will. Only then can they find accord.[26]

Had Alisoun acquiesced, though, she would have ceased to exist. It is her ranting and raving, her squabbling and dominance, her coarseness, her contrariness, and her manipulation of others that make her immortal today. Nor does peer pressure subdue her. Her clearly defined ego allows her to answer the Friar's complaints about her over-long prologue with a slur on his character in her tale. We cannot imagine that the Clerk's tale of Griselda, suited as it is to her own tale, would reduce the Wife to silence. Indeed, her last remarks to us are as impudent as her first. This unshakeable attitude provides the dramatic tension in her prologue, which is in fact a contest of wills—the divine will and her own.

There remains one last confession by a Canterbury pilgrim to consider: Chaucer's literary confession of sins in his Retraction. Here he deplores his works that "sownen into synne," blaming them on his ignorance of his craft and not on any specific intent to do evil ("arrette it to the defaute of myn unkonnynge, and nat to my wyl, that wolde full fayn have seyd bettre if I hadde had konnynge"). He promises to repent of any additional sinful writings, "if they were in my remembrance," and ends with a prayer for his own salvation. It is in this confession, fittingly placed after the Parson's treatise on penance, that Chaucer makes final use of the penitential tradition to add one last touch of modeling to the character of his naive narrator and to end his *Tales* on a note of proper gaiety.

The Retraction has always been a source of consternation among critics, mostly because they have believed it to be autobiographical and somber in tone. J. E. Wells has summarized the situation as follows: "The question of the authenticity of the passage is of importance . . . since it presents to us the strange picture of Chaucer, under what seems to be the pressure of narrow tenets, apologizing for and condemning most of what he had labored for in literature."[27] Scholars have often felt it necessary to invent a fiction to explain the ending of the poem. According to The Reverend Thomas Frognall Dibdin, the Retraction is not the work of Chaucer at all, but was written by his confessor (probably a monk of Westminster Abbey), who felt that he was carrying out the poet's last desire.[28] Father Herbert Thurston, having execrated Chaucer for "doing the devil's work," found some consolation in the knowledge that he had had the grace in the end to admit he had acted in "bad faith."[29]

Recent critics have also had trouble making sense of this last section of the poem. J. D. Gordon finds no evidence that Chaucer's works were thought so repugnant or scandalous during his lifetime as to require from him any kind of "public penance." Yet Gordon too envisions Chaucer as a cautious old man, doubting the propriety of his worldly works and choosing finally "the course of prudence."[30] For Donald Howard, Chaucer is practicing here the *ars moriendi*, as he "prepares for and embraces death after the manner of his age."[31] And John Gardner's *The Life and Times of Chaucer* ends with a "fictional reconstruction" of the poet writing his Retraction as an old man. Gardner "hears" Chaucer lament that he did not write poems to help men through death: "[he] should have written holy saints' lives, moving songs about the gentleness of Jesus, the foolishness of thinking all one's life about the world."[32] But the problem with the Retraction does not lie in Chaucer and the state of his mind at death, but rather in our traditional way of viewing the work, which is neither autobiographical nor solemn in tone. In fact, the penitential elements in this "confession" are as ironic as those which began with the Host in the General Prologue and continued throughout the entire poem.[33] An ironic reading is consistent with the tone of the work as a whole and with the personalities of the poet and the pilgrim as the reader has come to know them.

Chaucer has taken some pains to alert the audience that this last section of the *Tales* is spoken by his *persona*. To begin with, it reveals one of the most persistent traits of the narrator—his "ignorance and ineptness."[34] Over and over, the pilgrim maintains that he has no control over the other members of the group and the tales that they tell. He regrets that he must relate The Miller's Tale, but he does not do so "Of yvel entente" (I [A] 3173). He repeats Chauntecleer's pejorative comments about women but is quick to add, "Thise been the cokkes wordes, and nat myne" (VII, 3265). His own failure as a teller of tales is brought home forcefuly to him by Harry Bailly, who interrupts The Tale of Sir Thopas rudely:

> "Namoore of this, for Goddes dignitee,"
> Quod oure Hooste, "for thou makest me
> So wery of thy verray lewednesse."
>
> (B² 2109–11)

In addition to being "ignorant" and "inept," Chaucer the pilgrim is also naive and easily impressed by the words of the other pilgrims. This is why he admires the Prioress and thinks the Monk should be an abbot. And it is Chaucer the pilgrim who has been so swayed by the words of the Parson that he is willing to renounce all his literary sins, committed out of his "unkonnynge" ("[he] wolde ful fayn have seyd bettre if [he] hadde had konnynge"), for his "entente" was for the best.

In judging these "sins" and the "entente" behind the telling, we must not forget that Chaucer the pilgrim, and the persona in the other poems too, is also depicted as a poet. The introduction to The Man of Law's Tale contains the well-known passage in which the Sergeant laments the fact that Chaucer had already told the tales he himself wanted to tell, even though the poet had not done a particularly good job ("he kan but lewedly / On metres and on rymyng craftily" [II (B) 47–48]). The Sergeant then goes on to make specific reference to the Book of the Duchess (II [B¹] 57) and the Legend of Good Women (II [B¹] 61). In the Prologue to the latter poem, the god of love chastises Chaucer the persona for translating the Roman de la Rose and for telling "how that Crisseyde Troylus forsok" (G 265). One should not be surprised, then, to find all of these works also mentioned in the Retraction.

Another stylistic technique of Chaucer's that ultimately serves to link his Retraction with his persona is the sly planting of a word or phrase that will later on be found by the reader in another context. An example of this is Chaucer's use of the phrase "for pity renneth soone in gentil herte" in The Knight's Tale and again, in an entirely different context, in The Merchant's Tale. Also, the phrase "She leet no morsel from hir lippes falle," which is associated with the overindulgent Prioress, is given ironic overtones when the Nun's Priest says of the ascetic widow, "No deyntee morsel passed thurgh hir throte." And the key words in Chaucer's Retraction can be found earlier, at the ending of the Pilgrim's own tale of Melibee. In fact, these two sections, which are different from all the other endings in the Canterbury Tales, are so closely suited to one another that they form a dialogue on the subject of sin and repentance. Melibee, in the role of priest, has decided to forgive his enemies, but first he accuses them of "pride," "presumpcioun," "folie," "necligence and unkonnynge" (VII B^2 1876), precisely the sins of which the Retraction repents. Several times Melibee asks his enemies if they are "sory and repentant of [their] giltes" (VII B^2 3069 and 1884). The voice in the Retraction begs "foryeve me my giltes" (X [I] 1083). Melibee's God will forgive the truly repentant sinner "and bryngen [him] to the blisse that nevere hath ende" (VIII 1887). Here Chaucer the pilgrim brings his tale to an end, and when he speaks again he uses the same words in another way: to achieve this "blisse," he prays to be "oon of hem at the day of doom that shulle be saved." It is difficult to take the Retraction as that of Chaucer's own person when such similar words and ideas occur in a story told by his persona.

There is also good reason not to take the homiletic ending of the poem seriously. Throughout the *Tales*, Chaucer has found great sport in using the devotional ending with an ironic twist. Often, in fact, the contrast between a pilgrim's pious words and Chaucer's attitude toward that pilgrim is a source of humor. For example, the nefarious Friar prays innocently that "thise somonours hem repente/ Of hir mysdedes, er that the feend hem hente!" (III [D] 1663–64). The Wife of Bath signals the conclusion of her tale with the "prayer" that "Jhesu Crist us sende/ Housbondes meeke, yonge, and fressh abedde/ And grace t'overbyde hem that we wedde" (III [D] 1258–60). Because of the frequency of this kind of ending, Chaucer's audience would have been primed for it and attuned to the nuances of tone.

In an article entitled "Chaucer's 'Retractions': The Conclusion of the *Canterbury Tales* and Its Place in Literary Tradition," Olive Sayce has also been concerned with Chaucer's tone. She begins by discussing the retractions genre—a European, not an English tradition—and has found that Chaucer's work is perfectly in keeping with the norm. The common characteristics of such a genre include an ending with prayers, biblical quotations and parables, confessions of unworthiness and sin (including literary "sins"), expression of the desire to make amends by writing an edifying work, and mention of the poet's name and titles of his work.[35]

There is one particular way in which Sayce finds Chaucer's Retraction to be unique: it is humorous, and a close examination "forbids a straightforward reading as an expression of sincere repentance."[36] Chaucer's phrase "Al that is writen is writen for oure doctrine" is usually interpreted as a gloss upon 2 Timothy 3:16: *Omnis Scriptura divinitus inspirata utilis est ad docendum* [All Scripture, divinely inspired, is useful for teaching], which praises sacred works and condemns worldly fables. This reference is specifically cited by the Parson in the prologue to his tale. But Sayce suggests that Chaucer is alluding to Romans 15:4, where Paul, referring to the works of the Old Testament, states: *Quaecumque enim scripta sunt, ad nostram doctrinam scripta sunt* [For whatsoever indeed was written, was written for our instruction]. Thus, ironically, the poet is seen to be attesting to the value of his own worldly works. The precise listing of works that Chaucer condemns versus the vague reference to the works for which he is to be praised ("bookes of legendes of seintes, and omelies, and moralitee, and devocions") suggest that Chaucer was more interested in establishing a canon of his works than in retracting them. And, finally, the phrases "and many another book, if they were in my remembrance," and "many a leccherous lay" in reference to his own lyric poetry, are humorous allusions to the wording of confessional manauls and as such serve "to weaken the force of [Chaucer's] confession."[37]

When the Retraction is seen to be properly humorous and impersonal, the problem of autobiography—pious old Chaucer recanting his works before death—ceases to exist. "It would be extremely surprising to find that within this traditional framework, which is in no way personal, there occurred an autobiographical confession."[38] Even the rubric "Heere taketh the makere of this book his leve," which is usually cited in favor of an autobiographical read-

ing, fails to support such an interpretation. Rickart and
Manly state that this heading occurs only in fifteen of the
85½ manuscripts and was probably a scribal emenda-
tion.[39] And, finally, though such an ending seems incom-
patible with Chaucer the poet, it is perfectly in keeping
with the character of Chaucer the pilgrim as it has been
established throughout the *Tales*.

Chaucer's Retraction is a culmination of the penitential
motifs that the poet has been establishing since the beginning of the poem. Starting with the description of the
Host-priest in the General Prologue, moving on to a
parody of the circumstances in the prologue of the Canon's Yeoman, the listing of motives of the manuals in the
monologue of the impenitent Pardoner, and the "up-so-
doun" version of the priest and penitent in the Wife of
Bath's prologue, Chaucer has completed his poem and his
persona with a humorous recounting of the confession's
end. "And thus, in the manner which he has followed
throughout the *Tales*, he has with a flip of the wrist restored the balance of good humor, and while not detract-
ing from the worth of the [Parson's sermon], places it
within the context of optimistic humanity."[40] The modern
audience can never recapture Chaucer's tone as he read
his finest work to the lords and ladies of the court. But one
can hardly deny him here one last sly smile.

Chaucer's method shares certain constituent elements
of the sacrament with that of his contemporaries: a sinner,
knowledgeable about his sins, his motives, and the extent
of his guilt; a "priest" who interrogates his penitents, extracting from them the circumstances surrounding their
actions; the penitential manual used in part to probe for
sins; and, inevitably, a "confession."

But Chaucer is also different from his peers. He depicts
sinners who from the very beginning are knowledgeable
of their sinful acts. They understand the "process" of sinning and the matters of motive, intent, and will and do not
have to be probed and groped. The Canon's Yeoman and
Chaucer the pilgrim feel contrition over their sins, but the
Pardoner and the Wife of Bath are unrepentant through-

out. Some of Chaucer's most attractive sinners, in fact, luxuriate in their own sinfulness. Though they are able and willing to explain their evil deeds and motives to the group, they are thoroughly unrepentant. Furthermore, throughout their "confessions" the egos of these characters remain intact. Because they are never divested of their "selfness," they are a commanding presence for the duration of the *Canterbury Tales.*

Chaucer's innovativeness, then, lies in the way he humanizes those various faults and traits of sin which the penitential tradition had preached against for two hundred years, by providing a psychologically plausible context for sin to exist in. It is tenable that characters like the Pardoner and the Wife of Bath, ostentatious in dress and attitude, impudent and scornful in speech, would have excessive egos, which are naturally revealed whenever these characters are "onstage." As long as a character is allegorical or based on the "sin-knowledge-humility" formula, his capacity to impress us with the force of his ego is limited. But when there is no formula, no external set of strictures for a character to adhere to, then his being can be determined by his own internal complexities and he is limitless. In the *Canterbury Tales,* Chaucer the artist outgrew Chaucer the medieval moralist.[41] His sinners are the "best" sinners and, therefore, the "best" characters.

Despite Chaucer's innovations, however, his technique owes a substantial amount to that same penitential tradition which created the Poenitens, the sinful anchoresses, the unrepentant sinners of the penitential sermons. Ultimately, he is indebted to the synodalia of the thirteenth-century bishops for making public various points of the doctrine of sin, so that Chaucer and his audience might assimilate it; to the Schoolmen for clarifying problems of motive and the will; and, finally, to the *Omnis utriusque sexus* decree of 1215, which established confession as the dominant mode of discourse in medieval Christianity.

From a prospect in the early thirteenth century, no one could have imagined the effect of the *Omnis utriusque sexus* decree on the belletristic literature of the late Middle Ages.

It could not have been suspected that provisions to cleanse the members of the Church would contribute to the development of the fictional sinner. But by the fourteenth century, as we have seen, medieval poets were using their knowledge of the interior workings of sin gained from the confessional to create some of the richest characters of the Middle Ages, characters possessed of a depth and resonance that every real sinner in the audience could appreciate and know.

In 1215, Pope Innocent III was naturally unconcerned about such "by-products" as these. Instead, he and his bishops were confronted with the enormous task of setting right a penitential system that for hundreds of years had failed to produce the level of informed piety that a mentality of reform required, largely because its instigators had been more concerned with penance as a punishment for sins than with the psychology of the sinner himself. The reformed system took years to crystallize; clergy and laity alike, who had been mostly innocent of the doctrine, might be expected to have been slow to respond to the system of thrice-annual confession and elaborate instruction of the penitent within the confessional. But by the fourteenth century it was the property of all the faithful, almost a two-century-old tradition. It is, therefore, not surprising that medieval poets would make use of some facets of penitentialism in their works. The paradox is that out of the very confessional that had sought to suppress sin emerged the fictional sinner.

But the paradox should not be surprising. Confession, after all, did not teach about the mind of the saint, but about the intricate and convoluted mind of the sinner. This is what the priest drew from his penitent, what the poets learned from their own confessions, and what they could expect their audiences to understand. But there is another, more structural reason for the popularity of the sinner as a character. The process of depicting the perfect penitent in the confessional manuals is totally reductive; he is made completely humble and left with no personality traits that can be developed. Only the sinner has a clearly defined ego. He is rich, spontaneous, and alive because his will is attracted to a multitude of forbidden objects. As long as he remains sinful, and is not subdued, the sinner is able by his *engin* to energize both the plot and the characters around him.

In the thirteenth and fourteenth centuries, English Christianity possessed a cohesiveness, however troubled, that it was to lose in the Reformation. After the break with Rome, the Anglican Church abolished auricular confession. With it inevitably went the continual exposure to the psychology of sin available to all through the confessional, and the churchgoer had to find other agents for his instruction. Mandatory confession for all the faithful had lasted only a short time—only a few hundred years. Yet it is hard to imagine that the later Middle Ages would have made such progress in characterization had it not been for the penitential tradition. We shall never know, of course, what English literature would have been like without the *Omnis utriusque sexus* decree. But the poetry of the late Middle Ages in England is richer for expanding its repertoire, for adding to the saint and the hero the beleaguered soul of the sinner.

Notes

Introduction

1. Robert Mannyng, *Handlyng Synne, EETS* 119, 123, ed. Frederick J. Furnivall (London: Kegan Paul, Trench, Trubner & Co., 1901), pp. 369–70, ll. 11845–66. Subsequent references in the text.

2. *An Alphabet of Tales, EETS* 126–27, ed. Mary M. Banks (London: Kegan Paul, Trench, Trubner & Co., 1904), p. 145, ll. 3–17. Subsequent references in the text.

3. *Speculum Sacerdotale, EETS* 200, ed. Edward H. Weatherly (1936; reprint ed. New York: Kraus Reprint Co., 1971), pp. 59–60.

4. Robert W. Hanning, *The Individual in Twelfth-Century Romance* (New Haven and London: Yale University Press, 1977), p. 235.

5. This period-name to describe those poets who wrote during the reign of Richard II was formulated by John Burrow in *Ricardian Poetry* (New Haven, Conn.: Yale University Press, 1971).

6. Geoffrey Chaucer, *The Summoner's Tale*, in *The Works of Geoffrey Chaucer*, ed. F. N. Robinson, 2d ed. (Boston: Houghton Mifflin, 1957), ll. 1817–18. Subsequent references in the text.

7. For discussions of England at the time of the interdict and subsequent excommunication of John, see Sidney Painter, *The Reign of King John* (1949; reprint ed. Baltimore: The Johns Hopkins Press, 1964), pp. 151–202; Alan Lloyd, *The Maligned Monarch: A Life of King John of England* (New York: Doubleday & Company, 1972), pp. 142–63; John T. Appleby, *John, King of England* (New York: Alfred A. Knopf, 1959), pp. 151–218.

Chapter 1: The Genealogy of the Sinner: A Study in the Background of Penance

1. For treatments of early Christian penance, see Bernhard Poschmann, *Penance and the Anointing of the Sick*, trans. Francis Courtney (New York: Herder & Herder, 1964); Henry Charles Lea, *A History of Auricular Confessions and Indulgences in the Latin Church*, vol. 1 (Philadelphia: Lea Brothers & Co., 1896); Oscar D. Watkins, *A History of Penance*, vol. 1 (New York: Burt Franklin, 1961); O. Cullman, *The Earliest Chris-*

tian Confessions, trans. J. K. S. Reid (London: Lutterworth Press, 1949). See also "Penance," *The Catholic Encyclopedia,* 11th ed., ed. Charles G. Herbermann et al. (New York: The Encyclopedia Press, 1911); "Penance," *Sacramentum Mundi: An Encyclopedia of Theology,* ed. Karl Rahner et al. (New York: Herder & Herder, 1968–70).

2. The practice of treating penitents as criminals was continued at least up until the time of Augustine. In *Epistola* 153.3, *PL* 33, 670, Augustine remarks that secular courts often released criminals at the intercession of bishops on the promise that these criminals should be subject to penance. Lea states that the early Church "was framing a system of criminal jurisprudence and punished the criminal and if he refused [penance], ejected him from the Church" (1: 13 ff.).

3. This public demonstration, known as the *publicatio sui,* was necessary for forgiveness and was divided into five stages, the length of each depending on the enormity of the "crime" committed by the penitent. In the first stage, called the *fletus* or weeping, the individual stood outside the church during the Mass. When he progressed to the second stage, the *audio,* he was admitted to the porch of the church and allowed to hear the sermon, but he was compelled to leave before the beginning of the Mass proper. In the *substratio,* or kneeling stage, the penitent could hear the prayers, but he must lie down or kneel on the floor of the church. During the fourth stage, the *congregatio,* he remained with the faithful during the mysteries but was not allowed to partake. The final stage was the reconciliation (Lea, *Auricular Confessions,* 1: 24).

4. *De Poenitentia,* 2.50, 10.11, *PL,* 2,1.

5. Strangely enough, perhaps because of their isolation, the Celtic and Anglo-Saxon churches seemed to know nothing of the Continental teachings, which deemphasized both confession and the role of the priest and which involved a public penance that could not be repeated. See Poschmann, *Penance,* p. 124.

6. John T. McNeil and Helena M. Gamer, *Medieval Handbooks of Penance* (New York: Columbia University, 1938), p. 28.

7. McNeil and Gamer, *Medieval Handbooks,* p. 100. Hereafter abbreviated *MHP.* Subsequent references to penitentials in the text.

8. McNeil and Gamer, *MHP,* p. 28. See also Poschmann, *Penance,* pp. 138 ff. This confidentiality continued into the penances assigned by the priest, which often began and ended with prescribed exercises that the penitent was able to perform in private. The act itself usually involved fasting on bread and water. Later on, depending on the penitent's satisfactory performance, this became an abstinence from meat and wine (Watkins, *History of Penance,* 2: 611 and 616). If the sin had been of particular gravity, the penitent was often exiled and stripped of all possessions save a pilgrim's staff. Or he might be shut up in a monastery for the remainder of his life (Paul F. Palmer, ed., *Sacraments and Forgiveness: Sources of Christian Theology,* [London: Darton, Longman

& Todd, 1959], 2: 373). For a lesser sin, he might be assigned a certain number of psalms and genuflections or asked to spend several nights at the tomb of a saint, singing songs and reciting prayers (Cyrille Vogel, *Les "Libri Paenitentiales"* [Belgium: Brepols, 1978], p. 47).

9. Actually, the Celtic monks, many of whom had some knowledge of medicine, were often trained to think of sin as a disease and, accordingly, to treat the sinner as a sick patient in need of aid (see *MPH*, pp. 45–46). This metaphor can be extended. Both sin and sickness are infirmities and interior states. Both are mysterious in their workings, but if the exact remedy is made known they are curable. Just as different diseases require different remedies, there are also differentiations among states of sinfulness. Consequently, penances were often based on the medical theory of contraries, whereby a disease is cured by its opposite and a fault is replaced by its corresponding virtue. See John T. McNeil and Helena M. Gamer, "Medicine for Sin as Prescribed in the Penitentials," *Church History* 1 (1932): 14–26. More recent articles on this subject add little to the above.

10. Lea, *Auricular Confessions,* 1: 189.

11. "Pénitence, la reforme Carolingienne, la pratique," *Dictionnaire de Théologie Catholique,* ed. Emile Amann (Paris: Librairie Letouzey et Ane, 1933), 12: 1, col. 874. The king is not further identified.

12. Ibid., cols. 872–77.

13. Vogel, *"Libri Paenitentiales,"* p. 38.

14. For studies in Pope Innocent's ambience, see R. W. Southern, *The Making of the Middle Ages* (1953; reprint ed. New Haven: Yale University Press, 1967), pp. 219–57; Norman F. Cantor, *Medieval History: The Life and Death of a Civilization* (New York: MacMillan Co., 1969), pp. 335–75; Adolf Katzenellenbogen, *The Sculptural Programs of Chartres Cathedral* (New York: W. W. Norton & Co., 1959); Joseph Clayton, *Pope Innocent and His Times* (Milwaukee, Wis.: Bruce Publishing Co., 1941).

15. Watkins, *History of Penance,* p. 622.

16. There is no specific date on which penance "became" a sacrament. The *Sacramentum Mundi* states that, although the sacramental nature is clearly testified to during the patristic period, the term *sacrament* was not generally used (p. 393). Penance *was* considered a sacrament by the middle of the twelfth century, when sacraments were defined, and by the beginning of the thirteenth century the doctrine of penance was taken for granted (p. 395). However, the enumeration of the seven sacraments did not become part of Canon Law until the Council of Trent in the sixteenth century.

17. Joannes Dominicus Mansi, *Sacrorum Conciliorum, Nova et Amplissima Collecto* (Venice: Antonio Zatta, 1779), 22: 1010.

18. No clear agreement has been reached about the term "age of discretion." Evidence suggests that this age differed for girls and boys and could vary from person to person, because one had to have the

ability to discern right from wrong. Generally, confession seems to have begun somewhere between the ages of seven and fourteen (Thomas N. Tentler, *Sin and Confession on the Eve of the Reformation* [Princeton, N.J.: Princeton University Press, 1977], p. 70, n. 1).

19. Lea, *Auricular Confessions*, 1: 370 and 372–73.

20. *Cursor Mundi*, vol. 5, ed. Richard Morris, *EETS* 68 (London: Oxford University Press, 1966), p. 1514, ll. 27152–59. Erroneously cited by Morris as 21152. Subsequent references in the text.

21. Poschmann, *Penance*, p. 142.

22. Ibid., p. 176.

23. Lea, *Auricular Confessions*, 1: 218–19.

24. *The Clensyng of Mannes Soule*, ed. Walter K. Everett, Diss., University of North Carolina 1974, p. 17, ll. 3–8. As was generally the case, contemporary anecdotes helped this "doctrine" to spread. One thirteenth-century story collected by Caesar of Heisterbach tells of a priest who had committed adultery with the wife of a knight of the village, and though the latter suspected this he had no concrete proof. Learning that in a nearby town lived a man possessed of a demon so vile that in the presence of bystanders he would reveal sins not effaced by confession, the knight asked the priest to accompany him there. The priest could not refuse, but as they neared the town he became frightened and feared for his life when the demon should reveal his adultery. Thereupon, he asked the knight to follow him into a stable, where he fell upon his knees and begged that his confession be heard and penance be assigned to him. The knight agreed and did as he was told (*Translations and Reprints from the Original Sources of European History*, vol. 2, no. 4, ed. Dana C. Munro [Pennsylvania: P. S. King & Son, 1897], p. 14). Such tales captured the popular imagination and worked their way into the writings of later poets.

25. *Cambridge Medieval History*, ed. J. R. Tanner et al. (New York: The Macmillan Co., 1936), 6:691.

26. For a concise history of the concept of "intention" in ethics, see Anthony Kenny, *Anatomy of the Soul* (Oxford: Blackwell, 1973), pp. 129–47.

27. *Peter Abelard's "Ethics,"* ed. and trans. D. E. Luscombe (Oxford: Clarendon Press, 1971), pp. 44–47. Subsequent references in the text.

28. D. E. Luscombe, intro., *Peter Abelard's "Ethics,"* p. xxxii.

29. *Summa Theologica*, vol. 2, ed. T. Gilby (Cambridge: Blackfriars, 1964—), 2, q. 72, a. 8.

30. Ibid., a. 9.

31. "Sin, Theology of," *New Catholic Encyclopedia*, ed. Conde B. Pallen and John J. Wynne (New York: Universal Knowledge Foundation, 1929), 13:224.

32. "Contrition," *New Catholic Encyclopedia*, p. 281.

33. Thomas Aquinas, *Summae Suppl.* q. 9, a.4.

Chapter 2: Educating the Audience: The Sinner Emerges

1. "Ay whyle þey holde þe fryste sylabul,/ þe folghþe ys gode wythouten fabul" (John Mirk, *Instructions for Parish Priests, EETS* 31, ed. Edward Peacock [1898; reprint ed. New York: Kraus Reprint Co., 1975], ll. 577–78). The *Instructions* is a fifteenth-century manual with a thirteenth-century source. Subsequent references in the text.

2. See Walter Ullman, *The Individual in Medieval Society* (Baltimore, Md.: Johns Hopkins, 1966), pp. 106–7.

3. *OED,* s.v.

4. Thomas Tentler, *Sin and Confession*, quotes the admiring reaction of an early-seventeenth-century editor to a penitential manual known as the *Raymundina* of Raymond de Peñafort: "Rarely or never does [the author] rely on his own judgment; for he thought novelties and unique opinions ought perpetually to be avoided like the plague" (p. 32).

5. William de Montibus (or Willemus de Monte), a chancellor of Lincoln in the late twelfth century, wrote elementary instructions for the clergy and alphabetical *distinctiones*—consisting of a series of glossed verses on *Ascensio Christi, Angeli, Ascensus*, and the like. He also wrote similes as preaching aids, "little works on penance," and mistakes to avoid during church services. It is unlikely that any of these works survive. William's influence seems to have been felt mainly in the Midlands and east of England. After his death, the school he founded at Lincoln soon ceased to exist. However, a later thirteenth-century theologian named Richard de Wethringsette, a student of William, and the first-known chancellor of the University of Cambridge, presumably wrote a manual for priests known as the "Lumnia," based on a compilation from the *Summa* of William. None of these works would significantly affect the thirteenth century. See R. W. Hunt, "English Learning in the Late Twelfth Century," *Essays in Medieval History,* ed. R. W. Southern (London: Macmillan, 1968), pp. 108–9. See also Josiah C. Russell, *Dictionary of Writers of Thirteenth-Century England* (London: Longmans, Green & Co., 1936), pp. 196 and 124.

6. J. J. Francis Firth, intro. to *Robert of Flamborough: Liber Poenitentialis* (Toronto: Pontifical Institute of Mediaeval Studies, 1971), p. 18.

7. Robert of Flamborough, *Liber Poenitentialis,* ed. J. J. Francis Firth (Toronto: Pontifical Institute of Mediaeval Studies, 1971), pp. 58–59. Subsequent references in the text.

8. *Ancrene Wisse,* ed. J. R. R. Tolkien, *EETS* 249 (London: Oxford University Press, 1962), p. 142. Subsequent references in the text. Two letters from the MS *Corpus Christi College Cambridge 402.* and have been replaced by the ampersand and the period, respectively.

9. *The Clensyng of Mannes Soule,* p. 39. ll. 5–14.

10. C. R. Cheney, *Medieval Texts and Studies* (Oxford: Clarendon Press, 1973), p. 187. According to J. H. R. Mooreman, *Church Life in England in the Thirteenth Century* (Cambridge: Cambridge University

Press, 1945), this clerical ignorance is hardly surprising. In an entertaining account, Mooreman explains that, in the early thirteenth century, education of any sort for a priest was rare. Those who did attend schools received only a "general education," which included no specifically religious or theological instructions beyond what they might pick up from attending university sermons (pp. 95–108).

11. Clerical ignorance was often a subject for laughter. Geraldus Cambrensis amused himself by collecting examples of one priest who could not distinguish between Barnabas and Barabbas and of another who announced that the feast day of Jude would not be celebrated, "Since he is the one who crucified our Lord" (cited in Mooreman, *Church Life*, p. 90).

12. Marion Gibbs and Lane Lang, *Bishops and Reform: 1215–1272* (London: Oxford University Press, 1934), p. 108.

13. *Councils & Synods, With Other Documents Relating to the English Church*, A.D. *1205–1313*, ed. F. M. Powicke and C. M. Cheney, 2 vols. (Oxford: Clarendon Press, 1964), II:72.

14. Ibid., II:220. Subsequent references in the text.

15. For a detailed study of the influence of preaching on medieval literature, see George R. Owst, *Literature and Pulpit in Medieval England* (1933; reprint ed. New York: Barnes & Noble, 1961), and idem, *Preaching in Medieval England* (1926; reprint ed. New York: Viking, 1959).

16. W. A. Pantin, *The English Church in the Fourteenth Century* (Notre Dame: University of Notre Dame Press, 1962), pp. 189–219. Grosseteste himself wrote a Latin manual entitled *Templus Domini*, which treats of the articles of faith, the Ten Commandments, and the seven sacraments, especially confession. Other Latin manuals of the thirteenth century include the *Summa Theologiae* of Richard de Wetheringsette, which contains sections on the Creed, the Lord's Prayer, the articles of faith, the gifts of the spirit, virtues and vices, sacraments (especially penance), and the Ten Commandments. The *Monologuium* is a treatise on the virtues and vices for young preachers; the *Legiliquium*, a study of the Ten Commandments. These last two manuals are attributed to John of Wales. See Homer G. Pfander, "Some Medieval Manuals of Religious Instruction in England," *JEGP* 35 (1936), 243–58. The success of the bishops in popularizing the confessional education for the laity can be seen in the thirteenth-century French manual, *Manuel des péchés*, which was to become a model for *Handlyng Synne*.

17. W. Nelson Francis, ed., *The Book of Vices and Virtues, EETS* 217 (London: Oxford University Press, 1942), p. x.

18. On the date of this collection, see John E. Wells, *Manual of Writings in Middle English*, 4th suppl. (New Haven, Conn.: Yale University Press, 1929), p. 1266.

19. *Old English Homilies, EETS* 29 and 34, ed. and trans. Richard Morris (London: N. Tribner & Co., 1868), pp. 22–23. Subsequent references in the text.

20. Owst, *Literature and Pulpit*, p. 237.

21. *The Discovery of the Individual*: 1050–1200 (New York: Harper and Row, 1972), p. 10.

22. *Journal of Psychology and Theology* 1 (1973): 36.

23. *New Ways in Psychoanalysis* (New York: W. W. Norton & Co., 1939), p. 211.

24. "Guilt: Where Theology and Psychology Meet," *Journal of Psychology and Theology* 2 (1974): 24. A number of works deal with the similarities and differences between confession and psychotherapy, and the following is only a brief listing of some of the most relevant. B. Stevenson, "Confession and Psychotherapy," *Journal of Pastoral Care* 20 (1966): 10–15, notes the similarities: the patient comes in with insecurities and discusses inmost feelings with confidence; there is a general atmosphere of acceptance; the goal is release (catharsis); the patient learns to do what is "right." There are a number of important differences, however. Psychoanalysis is geared to deal with what lies in the conscious acts of will. The confessor does not allow transference—no personal relationship takes place. Confession centers on objective guilt, not subjective feelings. V. Worthen, "Psychotherapy and Catholic Confession," *Journal of Religion and Health* 13 (1974): 275–84, points out additional contrasts. The very nature of psychotherapy implies that man can determine his fate. While one is in confession, however, God of His own free will elects to impart grace. Unlike confession, psychotherapy has no predetermined ritual to fit all individuals; it is individually oriented. The priest sees sin as the cause of unhappiness; the psychotherapist sees sin (or "egocentrism") as the "end result of an involuntary process contrary to the individual's will." An objective of psychotherapy is a positive self-image. On the other hand, Andreas Snoeck, *Confession and Psychoanalysis* (Westminster, Md.: The Newman Press, 1964), comments that neurotic persons who have an unconscious urge to humiliate themselves are not helped by confession but use it to punish themselves (p. 126). Both the similarities and the differences in confession and psychology will be of importance in the analysis of the sinners in the following chapters. See also Paul Martin, "Sin, Guilt, and Mental Health: Confession and Restitution as Means of Therapy," *Christian Century* 92 (1921): 525–27; A. C. Outler, "Karl Menninger and the Dimensions of Sin," *Theology Today* 31 (1974): 59–61; L. B. Thomas, "Sacramental Confession and Some Clinical Concerns," *Journal of Religion and Health* 4 (1965): 345–53; James H. Vandervelt and Robert P. Odenwald, *Psychiatry and Catholicism* (New York: McGraw Hill, 1952).

25. Horney, *New Ways in Psychoanalysis*, p. 229.

26. Stanley E. Fish, *Surprised by Sin: The Reader in Paradise Lost* (New York: St. Martin's Press, 1967), p. 11. Fish here is discussing the audience of *Paradise Lost*, but his method can be applied to this aspect of medieval literature as well.

Chapter 3: *Confession as Characterization in the Literature of Fourteenth-Century England*

1. *Lay Folks Mass Book*, EETS 71, ed. Thomas F. Simmons (1879; reprint ed. London: Oxford University Press, 1968), p. 8,1.36.

2. Ibid., p. 124, 11. 7–9.

3. *The Babees Book*, EETS 32, ed. F. J. Furnivall (1868; reprint ed. New York: Greenwood Press, 1969), p. 303, 11. 153–54.

4. For the complete text of this poem, see *Religious Lyrics of the Fourteenth Century*, ed. Carleton Brown (Oxford: Clarendon Press, 1952), pp. 109–10.

5. For a discussion of the Franciscan doctrine of penance as a theme in medieval lyrics, see David L. Jeffrey, *The Early English Lyric & Franciscan Spirituality* (Lincoln: University of Nebraska Press, 1975), pp. 55–63 and passim.

6. Manuals generally covered the seven deadly sins, the seven sacraments, and the twelve points of shrift, to a greater or lesser degree, and often other points of doctrine as well.

7. Anonymous, *The Seven Points of True Wisdom (Orologium Sapientiae)*, ed. Karl Horstmann, *Anglia* 10 (1887): 328. This work is an early-fifteenth-century translation of a Latin devotional work by Henry Suso, written ca. 1334–48.

8. Jean-Charles Payen, *Le Motif du repentir dans la littérature française médiévalê* (Geneva: Librairie Droz, 1968), p. 232.

9. Ibid., pp. 236–37.

10. Ibid., p. 232.

11. "Pos de chanter m'es pres talenz," in *Répertoire métrique de la póesie des troubadours*, ed. Istvan Frank (Paris: Bibliothèque de l'Ecole des Hautes Etudes, 1953–57), pp. 44,7.

12. *Mediaeval Latin Lyrics*, ed. and trans. Helen Waddell (1929; reprint ed. Baltimore, Md.: Penguin Books, 1964), pp. 178–79.

13. *King Arthur's Death*, ed. Larry D. Benson (New York: Bobbs-Merrill Company, 1974), 1. 3400. For a discussion of penance in the Alliterative *Morte Arthure*, see William Matthews, *The Tragedy of Arthur: A Study of the Alliterative "Morte Arthure"* (Berkeley and Los Angeles: University of California Press, 1960).

14. Laȝamon, *Roman de Brute*, ed. Frederick Maddon (London: Society of Antiquaries, 1847), ll. 22751–54.

15. In *Medieval Drama*, ed. and trans. David Bevington (Boston: Houghton Mifflin Co., 1975), pp. 167–68, s.d. and ll. 61–62.

16. Ibid., p. 103, ll. 519–21.

17. *Service for Representing Adam*, p. 104, ll. 11561–66. See also Edelgard DuBruck, "The Theme of Self-Accusation in Early French Literature: Adam and Theophile," *Romania* 94 (1973): 410–18.

18. Jacobus de Voragine, *Golden Legend,* trans. Granger Ryan and Helmut Ripperger (New York: Arno Press, 1969), p. 139.

19. Ibid., p. 148.

20. Ibid., p. 721.

21. Lawrence Baldassaro, "Dante the Pilgrim: Everyman as Sinner," *Dante Studies,* 92 (1974), 67.

22. Dante Alighieri, *The Purgatorio,* trans. John D. Sinclair (1939; reprint ed. New York: Oxford University Press, 1975), pp. 402–3.

23. Ibid.

24. *Piers Plowman as a Fourteenth-Century Apocalypse* (New Brunswick, N.J.: Rutgers University Press, 1961), p. 114.

25. Greta Hort, *Piers Plowman and Contemporary Religious Thought* (New York: The MacMillan Co., 1936), p. 57.

26. In Book VI of the C-Text (William Langland, *The Vision of William Concerning Piers the Plowman, EETS* 54, ed. Walter W. Skeat, vol. 1 [London: Oxford University Press, 1886], ll. 45–50), Langland remarks that he makes his living by saying the Paternoster and the Psalms. Surely no one would pay a layman to do this, but Langland's reference to his wife and child indicates that he was not a priest. Neville Coghill suggests that he was a *tonsuratus,* or acolyte (*Langland: Piers Plowman* [London: Longmans, Green & Co., 1964], p. 16). All references to *Piers Plowman* are to the C-Text, as presumably Langland's final word on the subject, and to Skeat's edition. Subsequent references in the text.

27. John Burrow, "The Audience of *Piers Plowman," Anglia* 75 (1957): 373–84.

28. See respectively, *Piers Plowman, A Contribution to the History of English Mysticism,* trans. Marion and Elise Richards (London: T. Fisher Unwil, 1894), and *Middle English Literature: A Critical Study of the Romances, the Religious Lyrics, "Piers Plowman"* (London: Methuen Press, 1951), p. 243.

29. "The Role of the Quotations in *Piers Plowman," Speculum* 52 (1977): 80–99.

30. See specifically Canon 66 (Mansi), which warns that all sacraments must be administered freely.

31. "The Significance of Haukyn, Activa Vita, in *Piers Plowman," Review of English Studies* 25 (1949): 109.

32. For an opposing view, see Morton W. Bloomfield, "*Piers Plowman* and the Three Grades of Chastity," *Anglia* 76 (1958), 227–53. According to Bloomfield, "Will grows from an impotent observer-hermit into a questioning pilgrim in the course of the poem as he becomes more and more involved with the questions he raises and the worlds he participates in" (p. 227).

33. John H. Fisher, *John Gower, Moral Philosopher and Friend of Chaucer* (New York: New York University Press, 1964), notes that penance is a major theme in the *Mirour de l'omme* and *Vox Clamantis,* as well as in the *Confessio.* However, he does not go on to discuss this further.

34. The character of Genius has sources other than that of the penitential manual. In a recent article, Denise N. Becker notes Gower's debt both to Alain de Lille's *De planctu Naturae* and Jean de Meun's *Roman de la Rose* in creating Genius's dual role of moral teacher and priest. See "The Priesthood of Genius: A Study of the Medieval Tradition," *Speculum* 51 (1976): 277–91. However, Genius's character is modeled much more closely on that of the medieval confessor than has previously been noted.

35. John J. McNally ("The Penitential and Courtly Traditions in Gower's *Confessio Amantis*," in *Studies in Medieval Culture*, ed. John R. Somerfeldt [Kalamazoo: Western Michigan University, 1964], p. 75) notes that, despite their eventually antithetical aims, courtly and divine lovers share certain points in common. Both have an unsated desire for a union with the "beloved." It is the fear of separation that brings both to the confessional. Each has hopes that "by receiving the sacrament of penance he will receive the grace of his beloved" (p. 82). Both penitent and lover assume positions of inferiority in relation to the objects of their love, and both are made better by this act of love. Furthermore, at least two of Ovid's characteristics of courtly love can be adapted to the penitential code: "The metaphor of sin as a malady is paralleled by that of love as a malady, and the metaphor of sin as an object of combat is paralleled by that of love as a kind of battle" (p. 82).

36. Critics have noted this fact, but mostly in passing, and none have determined the extent of the *Confessio*'s debt either to the penitential tradition or to the handbooks of penance. See, for example, McNally, *Penitential and Courtly Traditions*, p. 79; Patrick J. Gallacher, *Love, the Word, and Mercury: A Reading of John Gower's "Confessio Amantis"* (Albuquerque: University of New Mexico Press, 1975), p. 12; William G. Dodd, *Courtly Love in Chaucer and Gower*, in *Harvard Studies in English*, (Gloucester, Mass.: Peter Smith, 1959), 1: 44–45; John B. Dwyer, "The Tradition of Medieval Manuals of Religious Instruction in the Poems of John Gower, with Special Reference to the Development of the Book of Virtues," Diss., University of North Carolina, Chapel Hill, 1950.

37. John Gower, *The English Works of John Gower*, ed. G. C. Macauley (London: Kegan Paul, Trubner & Co., 1900), 1, ll. 213–14. Subsequent references in the text.

38. Mirk's *Instructions* advises more moderately: have "godely speche" (l. 1585).

39. See n. 22 for chap. 2, above.

40. Gallacher, *Love, the Word, and Mercury*, p. 188.

41. *Patience*, ed. J. J. Anderson (New York: Barnes & Noble, 1969), l. 74. (Erroneously cited by Anderson as line 78.) Subsequent references in the text.

42. Aquinas, *ST* 3a, 48.2.

43. The description of the penance of the Ninevites is strongly reminiscent of the *publicatio sui* practiced on the Continent before the in-

troduction of the Celtic penance in the sixth century (see n. 3 of chap. 1, above). If the poet expected his audience to find these measures familiar, then the poem was most likely written for the clergy. For a discussion of the poem's audience, see Ordelle G. Hill, "The Audience of *Patience*," *Modern Philology* 66 (1968): 103–9.

44. A. C. Spearing, "*Patience* and the *Gawain*-Poet," *Anglia* 84 (1966): 316. Spearing remarks that "it is perhaps [God's] mercy even more than the power that reduces [Jonah] to absurdity.He is not destroyed by the storm, but protected in the midst of it; he is not even allowed to die defiantly" (p. 320).

45. *Cleanness*, in *Early English Alliterature Poems, EETS* 1, ed. Richard Harris (1864, reprint ed. London: Oxford University Press, 1933), 11. 1127–28. The poem contains a number of sinful characters, but, as Belshazzar is the most fully conceived, the part dealing with him is most relevant to this study. Subsequent references in the text.

46. *Pearl*, ed. E. V. Gordon (Oxford: Clarendon Press, 1974), 11. 282–84. Subsequent references in the text.

47. See Gordon M. Shedd, "Knight in Tarnished Armour: The Meaning of *Sir Gawain and the Green Knight*," *Modern Language Review* 62 (1976): 3–13; A. Francis Soucy, "Gawain's Fault: 'Angardez Pryde,'" *Chaucer Review* 13 (1978): 166–76; Michael Foley, "Gawain's Two Confessions Reconsidered," *Chaucer Review* 9 (1974): 73–79; John Burrow, "The Two Confession Scenes in *Sir Gawain and the Green Knight*," *Modern Philology* 57 (1959–60): 73–79; Nicolas Jacobs, "Gawain's False Confession," *English Studies* 51 (1970): 433–35.

48. See Robert Ackerman, "Penitential Doctrine and Gawain's Shield," *Anglia*, 76 (1958), 254-65.

49. John Burrow, *A Reading of "Sir Gawain and the Green Knight"* (1965; rept. London: Routledge, 1977).

50. *Sir Gawain and the Green Knight*, 2d ed., ed. J. R. R. Tolkien and E. V. Gordon (Oxford: Clarendon Press, 1968), 11. 311–12. Subsequent references in the text.

51. Burrow, *A Reading of "Sir Gawain and the Green Knight*," p. 154, sees Gawain's meeting with the Green Knight as a necessary *public* confession of guilt.

Chapter 4: Penitential Irony: A Look at Chaucer's Prologues

1. Judson B. Allen, "The Old Way and the Parson's Way: An Ironic Reading of the *Parson's Tale*," *Journal of Medieval and Renaissance Studies* 3 (1973): 260.

2. *PMLA* 29 (1914): 93–128.

3. John Livingston Lowes, "Chaucer and the Seven Deadly Sins," *PMLA* 30 (1915): 251–52.

4. Ibid., p. 263.

5. Ibid., p. 258.

6. Christian K. Zacher, *Curiosity and Pilgrimage: The Literature of Four-teenth-Century England* (Baltimore and London: The John's Hopkins University Press, 1976), p. ix.

7. Ibid., p. 7.

8. W. F. Bryan and Germaine Dempster, in *Sources and Analogues of Chaucer's Canterbury Tales* (1941; reprint ed. New York: Humanities Press, 1958), pp. 723–60, suggest that the tale is derived from "De poenitentiis et remissionibus" in the *Summa* of Raymond de Peñaforte and from the *Summa vitiorum* of Peraldus. H. G. Pfander ("Some Medieval Manuals of Religious Instruction;" p. 254, n. 30) seems to have been the first to label this tale a "manual." Previously, it had been referred to as a sermon.

9. Jonathan Sumption, *Pilgrimage: An Image of Mediaeval Religion* (To-towa, N.J.: Rowman and Littlefield, 1975), p. 150. Sumption does not elaborate.

10. *Modern Language Quarterly* 31 (1970): 298–307.

11. Medieval confession was traditionally held in the open, presum-ably to avoid the suspicion of evil. The confessional (box) was not used until the middle of the sixteenth century. See Tentler, *Sin and Con-fession,* p. 82.

12. "Flock," s.v., *A Concordance to the Complete Works of Chaucer,* ed. John S. Tatlock and Arthur G. Kennedy (Washington, D.C.: The Car-negie Institute, 1927).

13. S. McCracken, "Confessional Prologues and the topography of the Canon's Yeoman," *Modern Philology* 68 (1971): 91.

14. See, for example, George M. Rulter, "Confession in Medieval Literature," Diss., Harvard University, 1929, p. 256. See also Laurence V. Ryan, "The Canon's Yeoman's Desperate Confession," *Chaucer Re-view* 8 (1974): 299.

15. Ryan, "Canon's Yeoman's Desperate Confession," p. 299. Ryan also notes that the Host examines the Yeoman about the religion of alchemy in a way that is "like a parody of the formula for questioning enjoined upon confessors," but he does not elaborate.

16. Ryan, "Canon's Yeoman's Desperate Confession," p. 306.

17. John Gardner, "The Canon's Yeoman's Prologue and Tale: An Interpretation," *Philological Quarterly,* 46 (1967), 2, n. 1.

18. Robert P. Miller, "Chaucer's Pardoner, the Scriptural Eunuch, and the Pardoner's Tale," *Speculum,* 30 (1955).

19. The words of Faux-Semblant are not a "confession" in the sense of the word employed here, although the character does use his speech to reveal his own sin of hypocrisy. But Jean de Meun, writing in the latter part of the thirteenth century, either did not, or could not, manipulate the subtle nuances of the confessional language to shape the complex character of the sinner. Instead, Faux-Semblant is simply a *type*, a moral abstraction. See John V. Fleming, *The "Roman de la Rose": A Study in Allegory and Iconography* (Princeton, N.J.: Princeton University

Press, 1969), pp. 161–70, and passim. For a brief discussion of "characterization" in Jean de Meun, see Charles Muscatine, *Chaucer and the French Tradition* (1957); reprint ed. Berkeley: University of California Press, 1973), pp. 71–97.

20. The word *entente* is an important one in Chaucer's works. See, for example, Richard Passon, " 'Entente' in Chaucer's Friar's Tale," *Chaucer Review* 2 (1967): 166–71. Passon comments on the regular use of this word in the tale—six occurrences in 360 lines. He discusses the theological dimensions of the word and its use in furthering the plot of that tale, a use that convinces Passon that the tale is not a fabliau, but an exemplum.

21. Charles Mitchell, "The Moral Superiority of Chaucer's Pardoner," *College English* 27 (1966): 437–44.

22. The *Lay Folks Mass Book* states:

> If þou be owte of charyte,
> þen is gode of god to craue,
> þat þou charyte may haue.
> þere when þo prest [þo] pax wil kis,
> Knele þou & praye þen þis.
>
> (P. 49, 11. 511–15)

In the *Parson's Tale*, the Parson cites as an example of pride the failure to "kisse pax" (X [I] 407).

23. "Chaucerian Confession: Penitential Literature and the Pardoner," *Medievalia et Humanistica*, n.s. 7 (1976): 16.

24. In *Studies in Medieval Literature in Honor of Professor Albert C. Baugh,* ed. MacEdward Leach (Philadelphia: University of Pennsylvania Press, 1961), p. 54.

25. St. Ambrose, *Expositionis in Lucam*, 8. 3 (*PL* 15, [1856]): "pugna atque dissensio est, quae non est a Deo, quia Deus charitas est."

26. On the Wife's failure to adhere to the Church's doctrine of marriage and her subsequent inability to achieve a state of grace, see James W. Cook, " 'That She was out of alle Charitee': Point-Counterpoint in the Wife of Bath's Prologue and Tale," *Chaucer Review* 13 (1978): 51–65.

27. Wells, *Manual of Writings in Middle English*, p. 747.

28. *Typographical Antiquities,* ed. Joseph Ames (London: Miller, 1810–19), 1: 294.

29. "The Conversion of Boccaccio and Chaucer," *Studies: An Irish Quarterly Review of Letters, Philosophy, and Science* 25 (1936): 215.

30. Gordon, "Chaucer's Retraction," pp. 92–94.

31. *The Idea of the Canterbury Tales* (Berkeley: University of California Press, 1976), p. 172.

32. John Gardner, *The Life and Times of Chaucer,* (Alfred A. Knopf: New York, 1977), p. 313. See also Rodney Delasanta, "Penance and Poetry in the *Canterbury Tales*," *PMLA* 93, no. 2 (1978): 242–43: "I find it

wholly appropriate that Chaucer the pilgrim—perhaps, too, Chaucer the poet—should himself be moved to formal penitential posture . . . and to expiative reaction of whatever may have offended—even unwillingly—over the course of a long and mixed career."

33. Several recent critics have noted that the *Parson's Tale*, which always precedes the Retraction, is also ironic. See Allen, "The Old Way and the Parson's Way," p. 260. See also John Finlayson, "The Satiric Mode and the *Parson's Tale*," *Chaucer Review* 6 (1971); 94–116.

34. A. C. Campbell, "Chaucer's 'Retraction': Who Retracted What?" *Revue de l'Université d'Ottawa*, 35 (1965), 41.

35. Olive Sayce, "Chaucer's 'Retractions': The Conclusion of the *Canterbury Tales* and Its Place in Literary Tradition," *MÆ* 40 (1971): 231.

36. Ibid., p. 245.

37. Ibid., p. 145.

38. Ibid., p. 237.

39. John M. Manly and Edith Rickart, *The Text of the Canterbury Tales, Studied on the Basis of All Known Manuscripts* (Chicago: University of Chicago Press, 1940), 3: 454, 471.

40. Campbell, "Chaucer's 'Retraction,' " p. 53.

41. See Alfred David, *The Strumpet Muse: Art and Morals in Chaucer's Poetry* (Bloomington & London: Indiana University Press, 1976), David contends that the "practice of poetry involved Chaucer in a constant effort to reconcile his obligations as a medieval author with his own artistic vision" (p. 5); yet David feels that for Chaucer such a reconciliation was ultimately impossible, and the poet finally put his writing aside. Therefore, David sees the Retraction as a sincere goodbye to the poetry that Chaucer still loves but at last repudiates.

Bibliography

The following abbreviations have been used in this study:

EETS   Early English Text Society
ELH   English Literary History
MÆ   Medium Aevum
JEGP   Journal of English and Germanic Philology
PMLA   Publications of the Modern Language Association
PL   Patrologiae, Series Latina

Primary Sources

Abelard, Peter. *Ethics.* Edited and translated by D. E. Luscombe. Oxford: Clarendon Press, 1971.

———. "In Parasceve Domini: III. Nocturno." In *Mediaeval Latin Lyrics.* Edited and translated by Helen Waddell. 1929; reprint ed. Baltimore, Md.: Penguin Books, 1964.

Alighieri, Dante. *The Inferno.* Translated by John D. Sinclair. 1939; reprint ed. New York: Oxford University Press, 1974.

———. *The Purgatorio.* Translated by John D. Sinclair. 1939; reprint ed. New York: Oxford University Press, 1975.

An Alphabet of Tales. Vols. 1 and 2. *EETS* 126–27. Edited by Mary M. Banks. 1904; reprint ed. New York: Kraus Reprint Co., 1975.

Ambrose, Saint. *De Poenitentia. PL* 1. Edited by J. T. Migne. Paris, 1878.

———. *Expositionis in Lucam. PL* 15. Edited by J. T. Migne. Paris, 1856.

Ancrene Wisse. Edited by J. R. R. Tolkien. *EETS* 249. London: Oxford University Press, 1962.

Aquinas, Saint Thomas. *Summa Theologiae*. Edited by T. Gilby. Cambridge: Blackfriars, 1964—.

Augustine, Saint. *De Diversis Quaestionibus*. *PL* 40. Edited by J. F. Migne. Paris, 1878.

———. *Epistola*. *PL* 33. Edited by J. F. Migne. Paris, 1878.

The Babees Book. *EETS* 32. Edited by Frederick J. Furnivall. 1868; reprint ed. New York: Greenwood Press, 1969.

Chaucer, Geoffrey. *The Canterbury Tales*. In *The Works of Geoffrey Chaucer*, edited by F. N. Robinson. Boston: Houghton Mifflin Co., 1957.

Cleanness in *Early English Alliterative Poems*. *EETS* 1. Edited by Richard Morris. 1864; reprint ed. London: Oxford University Press, 1921.

The Clensyng of Mannes Soule. Edited by Walter K. Everett. Dissertation, University of North Carolina, 1974.

Councils & Synods, With Other Documents Relating to the English Church: A.D. 1205–1313. 2 vols. Edited by F. M. Powicke and C. M. Cheney. Oxford: Clarendon Press, 1964.

Cursor Mundi. Vol. 5. Edited by Richard Morris. *EETS* 68. 1878; reprint ed. London: Oxford University Press, 1966.

Dan Michel. *Ayenbite of Inwyt*. *EETS* 23. 1866; reprint ed. New York: Kraus Reprint Co., 1975.

Didache. In *Les Ecrits des Pères Apostoliques*. Edited by François Louvel. Paris: Les Editions du Clef, 1963.

Flamborough, Robert of. *Liber Poenitentialis*. Toronto: Pontifical Institute of Mediaeval Studies, 1971.

Gower, John. *The English Works of John Gower*. Vols. 1 and 2. Edited by G. C. Macauley. London: Kegan Paul, Trubner & Co., 1900.

Guillaume IX. "Pos de chantar m'es pres talenz." In *Repertoire métrique de la poésie des troubadours*. Edited by Istvan Frank. Paris: Bibliothèque de l'Ecole des Hautes Etudes, 1953–57.

Hermas, le Pasteur. *Visio II*. In *Sources Chrétiennes*, vol. 53. Edited by Robert Joly. Paris: Les Editions du Clef, 1958.

Jacob's Well. vol. 1, Edited by Arthur Brandeis. *EETS* 115. 1900; reprint ed. New York: Kraus Reprint Co., 1975.

King Arthur's Death. Edited by Larry D. Benson. New York: New York: Bobbs-Merrill Company, 1974.

Langland, William. *The Vision of William Concerning Piers the Plowman.* Vols. 1 and 2. Edited by Walter W. Skeat. *EETS* 54. London: Oxford University Press, 1886.

The Lay Folks Mass Book. Edited by Thomas F. Simmons *EETS* 71. 1879; reprint ed. London: Oxford University Press, 1968.

Laȝamon. *Roman de Brute.* Edited by Frederic Maddon. London: Society of Antiquaries, 1847.

McNeil, John T. and Gamer, Helena M. *Medieval Handbooks of Penance.* New York: Columbia University, 1938.

Mannyng, Robert. *Handlyng Synne.* Edited by Frederick J. Furnivall. *EETS* 119 and 123. London: Kegan Paul, Trench, Trubner & Co., 1901.

Mediaeval Latin Lyrics. Edited by Helen Waddell. 1929; reprint ed. Baltimore, Md.: Penguin Books, 1964.

Middle English Dictionary. Edited by Sherman M. Kuhn. Ann Arbor: University of Michigan Press, 1963.

Mirk, John. *Instructions for Parish Priests.* Ed. Edward Peacock. *EETS* 31 (1898); reprint ed. New York: Kraus Reprint Co., 1975.

Old English Homilies. Edited by Richard Morris. *EETS* 29 and 34. London: N. Tribner & Co., 1867.

Oxford English Dictionary. Edited by James A. H. Murray, et al. Oxford: Clarendon Press, 1933.

Patience. Edited by J. J. Anderson. New York: Barnes & Noble, 1969.

Pearl. Edited by E. V. Gordon. Oxford: Clarendon Press, 1953.

Pseudo-Augustine. *De Vera et Falsa Poenitentia. PL* 42. Edited by J. F. Migne. Paris, 1878.

Religious Lyrics of the Fourteenth Century. Edited by Carleton Brown. Oxford: Clarendon Press, 1952.

Le Roman de la Rose. Edited by Ernest Langlois. 5 vols. Paris: Société des anciens textes français, 1914–1924.

"The *Romance of Thebes*: A Translation of the *Roman de Thebes*, Lines 1–5172." Translated by John S. Coley. Dissertation, Vanderbilt University, 1965.

Sacraments and Forgiveness: Sources of Christian Theology. Vol. 2. Edited by Paul F. Palmer. London: Darton, Longman & Todd, 1959.

Sacrorum Conciliorum, Nova et Amplissima Collectio, vol. 22. Edited by Joannes Dominicus Mansi. Venice Antonio Zatta, 1779.

The Service for Representing Adam. In *Medieval Drama,* edited by David Bevington. Boston: Houghton Mifflin, 1975. Pp. 81–121.

The Service for Representing the Conversion of The Blessed Apostle Paul. In *Medieval Drama,* edited by David Bevington. Boston: Houghton Mifflin, 1975. Pp. 165–68.

The Seven Points of True Wisdom [Orologium Sapientiae]. Edited by Karl Horstmann. *Anglia* 10 (1887): 323–89.

Sir Gawain and the Green Knight. Edited by J. R. R. Tolkien and E. V. Gordon. Oxford: Clarendon Press, 1968.

Speculum Sacerdotale. Edited by Edward H. Weatherly. *EETS* 200. 1936; reprint ed. New York: Kraus Reprint Co., 1971.

Tertullian. *De Poenitentia. PL* 1. Edited by J. F. Migne. Paris, 1878.

Translations and Reprints from the Original Sources of European History. Vol. 2, no. 4. Edited by Dana C. Munro. Pa.: P. S. King & Son, 1897.

Voragine, Jacobus de. *The Golden Legend.* Translated by Granger Ryan and Helmut Ripperger. New York: Arno Press, 1969.

Secondary Sources

Ackerman, Robert. "Penitential Doctrine and Gawain's Shield." *Anglia* 76 (1958): 254–65.

Alford, John A. "The Role of the Quotations in *Piers Plowman.*" *Speculum* 52 (1977): 80–99.

Allen Emily H. "On the Author of the *Ancrene Riwle. PMLA* 3 (1929): 635–81.

Allen, Judson B. "The Old Way and the Parson's Way: An Ironic Reading of the Parson's Tale." *Journal of Medieval and Renaissance Studies* 3 (1973): 255–71.

Appleby, John T. *John, King of England.* New York: Alfred A. Knopf, 1959.

Baldassaro, Lawrence. "Dante the Pilgrim: Everyman as Sinner." *Dante Studies* 92 (1974): 63–76.

Becker, Denise N. "The Priesthood of Genius: A Study of the Medieval Tradition." *Speculum* 51 (1976): 277–91.

Bennett, Henry S. *Life on the English Manor, 1150–1400.* Cambridge: Cambridge University Press, 1937.

Binns, L. Elliot. *Innocent III.* London: Methuen & Co., Ltd., 1931.

Bloomfield, Morton W. *"Piers Plowman* and the Three Grades of Chastity." *Anglia* (1958), pp. 227–53.

———. *Piers Plowman as a Fourteenth-Century Apocalypse.* New Brunswick, N.J.: Rutgers University Press, 1962.

———. *The Seven Deadly Sins.* East Lansing: Michigan State University Press, 1967.

Blythe, Joan Heiger. "Images of Wrath: Lydgate and Langland." Dissertation, University of North Carolina, 1971.

Booth, Wayne C. *The Rhetoric of Fiction.* Chicago & London: University of Chicago Press, 1961.

Brandt, William J. *The Shape of Medieval History.* New Haven & London: Yale University Press, 1966.

Browning, D. S. "Doctrine of Atonement Informed by the Psychotherapic Process." *Journal of Pastoral Care,* 17 (1963): 136–47.

Bryan, W. F., and Dempster, Germaine, eds. *Sources and Analogues of Chaucer's Canterbury Tales.* 1941; reprint ed. New York: Humanities Press, 1958.

Burrow, John A. "The Action of Langland's Second Vision." *Essays in Criticism* 15 (1965): 247–68.

———. "The Audience of *Piers Plowman." Anglia* 75 (1957): 373–84.

———. *A Reading of "Sir Gawain and the Green Knight."* 1965 reprint ed. London: Routledge & Kegan Paul, 1977.

———. *Ricardian Poetry: Chaucer, Gower, Langland and the "Gawain" Poet.* New Haven, Conn.: Yale University Press, 1971.

———. "The Two Confession Scenes in *Sir Gawain and the Green Knight." Modern Philology* 57 (1959–60): 73–79.

Cambridge Medieval History. Edited by J. R. Tanner et al. 1929; reprint ed. Cambridge: University Press, 1964.

Campbell, A. P. "Chaucer's 'Retraction'; Who Retracted What?" *Revue de l'Université d'Ottawa* 35 (1965), 35–53.

Cantor, Norman F. *Medieval History: The Life and Death of a Civilization.* New York: Macmillan Co., 1969.

The Catholic Encyclopedia. Ed. Charles G. Herbermann et al. New York: The Encyclopedia Press, 1911.

Cheney, C. R. *Medieval Texts and Studies.* Oxford: Clarendon Press, 1973.

Clayton, Joseph. *Pope Innocent and His Times.* Milwaukee, Wis.: The Bruce Publishing Co., 1941.

Coghill, Nevill. *Piers Plowman.* London: Longmans, Green, & Co., 1964.

A Concordance to the Complete Works of Chaucer. Edited by John S. P. Tatlock and Arthur G. Kennedy. Washington, D. C.: The Carnegie Institute, 1927.

"Confession, Frequency of." *New Catholic Encyclopedia.* 1969 edition.

"Confession, Seal of." *New Catholic Encyclopedia.* 1969 edition.

Cook, James W. "'That She was out of all Charitee': Point-Counterpoint in the Wife of Bath's Prologue and Tale." *Chaucer Review* 13 (1978): 51–65.

Coulton, G. C. *Medieval Studies.* First Series. London: Cambridge University Press, 1919.

Cowdrey, H. J. *The Cluniacs and the Gregorian Reform.* Oxford: Clarendon Press, 1970.

Cullmann, O. *The Earliest Christian Confessions.* Translated by J. K. S. Reid. London: Lutterworth Press, 1949.

Cutler, A. C. "Karl Menninger and the Dimensions of Sin." *Theology Today* 31 (1974): 59–61.

Cutts, Edward L. *Parish Priests and Their People in the Middle Ages in England.* 1898; reprint ed. New York: AMS Press, 1970.

David, Alfred. *The Strumpet Muse.* Bloomington: Indiana University Press, 1976.

Delasanta, Rodney. "Penance and Poetry in the *Canterbury Tales.*" *PMLA* 93, no. 2 (1978): 240–47.

———. "The Theme of Judgment in *The Canterbury Tales.*" *Modern Language Quarterly* 31 (1970): 298–307.

Dictionnaire de Théologie Catholique. Edited by Emile Amann. Paris: Librairie Letouzey et Ane, 1933.

Dodd, William G. *Courtly Love in Chaucer and Gower. Harvard Studies in English.* Vol. 1. Gloucester, Mass. Peter Smith, 1959.

Donaldson, E. Talbot. *Piers Plowman: The C-Text and Its Poet.* New Haven, Conn.: Yale University Press, 1949.

Du Bruck, Edelgard. "The Theme of Self-Accusation in Early French Literature: Adam and Theophile."*Romania* 94 (1973): 410–18.

Dwyer, John B. "The Tradition of Medieval Manuals of Religious Instruction in the Poems of John Gower, with Special Reference to the Development of the *Book of Virtues.*" Dissertation, University of North Carolina, 1950.

Egger, D. "De praxi paenitentiali Victorinorum." *Angelicum* 17 (1940): 156–79.

Finlayson, John. "The Satiric Mode and the Parson's Tale." *Chaucer Review* 6 (1971): 94–116.

Firth, J. J. Francis. Introduction to *Robert of Flamborough, Liber Poenitentialis.* Toronto: Pontifical Institute of Mediaeval Studies, 1971.

Fish, Stanley E. *Surprised by Sin: The Reader in Paradise Lost.* New York: St. Martin's Press, 1967.

Fisher, John A. *John Gower: Moral Philosopher and Friend of Chaucer.* New York: New York University Press, 1964.

Fleming, John V. *The "Roman de la Rose": A Study in Allegory and Iconography.* Princeton, N. J.: Princeton University Press, 1969.

Foley, Michael. "Gawain's Two Confessions Reconsidered." *Chaucer Review* 9(1974): 73–79.

Fowler, H. W. *A Dictionary of Modern English Usage.* London: Oxford University Press, 1946.

Francis, W. Nelson, ed. *The Book of Vices and Virtues.* EETS 217. London: Oxford University Press, 1942.

Frank, Robert W. *Piers Plowman and the Scheme of Salvation.* New Haven, Conn.: Shoe String Press, 1969.

Frantzen, Allen J. "The Keys of Heaven: Penance, Penitentials, and the Literature of Early Medieval England." Dissertation, University of Virginia, 1976.

Gallacher, Patrick J. *Love, the Word, and Mercury: A Reading of John Gower's 'Confessio Amantis,'* Albuguerque: University of New Mexico Press, 1975.

Gardner, John. "The Canon's Yeoman's Prologue and Tale: An Interpretation." *Philological Quarterly* 46 (1967): 1–17.

———. *The Life and Times of Chaucer.* New York: Alfred A. Knopf, 1977.

Gibbs, Marion and Lang, Lane. *Bishops and Reform: 1215–1272.* London: Oxford University Press, 1934.

Gillie, Christopher. *Character in English Literature.* New York: Barnes & Noble, 1965.

Gordon, J. D. "Chaucer's Retraction: A Review of Opinion." In *Studies in Medieval Literature in Honor of Professor Albert C. Baugh.* Edited by MacEdward Leach. Philadelphia: University of Pennsylvania Press, 1961. pp. 81–96.

Griffin, Mary. *Studies on Chaucer and His Audience.* Quebec: Les Editions L'Eclair, 1956.

Gunstone, John. *The Liturgy of Penance.* London: The Faith Press, 1966.

Hammes, John A. "The Christian in the Age of the Id." *Journal of Psychology and Theology* 1 (1973): 34–37.

Hanning, Robert W. *The Individual in Twelfth-Century Romance.* New Haven and London: Yale University Press, 1977.

Hill, Ordelle G. "The Audience of Patience." *Modern Philology* 66 (1968): 103–9.

Hill, Rosalind. "Public Penance: Some Problems of a Thirteenth-Century Bishop." *History*, n.s. 36 (1951): 213–26.

Hinnebusch, William A. *The Early English Friars Preachers.* Rome: Institute Storico Dominicano, 1951.

Hoben, Sr. Marian W. "John Gower's *Confessio Amantis*: A Critical Assessment of Theme and Structure." Dissertation, University of Wisconsin, 1969.

Horney, Karen. *New Ways in Psychoanalysis.* New York: W. W. Norton & Co., 1939.

Hort, Greta. *Piers Plowman and Contemporary Religious Thought.* New York: The Macmillan Co., 1936.

Howard, Donald R. *The Idea of the Canterbury Tales.* Berkeley: University of California Press, 1976.

Hughes, Phillip. *History of the Church.* Vol. 2. New York: Sheed & Ward, 1935.

Hunt, R. W. "English Learning in the Late Twelfth Century." In *Essays in Medieval History*, edited by R. W. Southern. London: Macmillan, 1968. Pp. 106–28.

Jacobs, Nicolas. "Gawain's False Confession." *English Studies*, 51 (1970); 433–35.

Jeffrey, David L. *The Early English & Franciscan Spirituality*. Lincoln: University of Nebraska Press, 1975.

Jusserand, J. J. *Piers Plowman: A Contribution to the History of English Mysticism*. Translated by Marion and Elise Richards. London: T. Fisher Unwin, 1894.

Kane, George. *Middle English Literature: A Critical Study of the Romances, the Religious Lyrics, "Piers Plowman."* London: Methuen, 1951.

Katzenellenbogen, Adolf. *The Sculptural Programs of Chartres Cathedral*. New York: W. W. Norton & Co., 1959.

Kenny, Anthony. *Anatomy of the Soul*. Oxford: Blackwells, 1973. Pp. 129–47.

Kuttner,   Stephen. "Pierre de Roissy and Robert of Flamborough." *Traditio* 2 (1944): 492–99.

Lea, Henry Charles. *A History of Auricular Confessions and Indulgences in the Latin Church*. Vols. 1 and 2. Philadelphia: Lea Brothers & Co., 1986.

Leclercq, Jean. "Modern Psychology and the Interpretation of Medieval Texts." *Speculum* 48 (1973): 476–90.

Lewis, C. S. *Allegory of Love: A Study in Medieval Tradition*. Oxford: Clarendon Press, 1938.

Lloyd, Alan. *The Maligned Monarch: A Life of King John of England*. New York: Doubleday & Co., 1972.

Lowes, John Livingston. "Chaucer and the Seven Deadly Sins." *PMLA* 30 (1915): 237–371.

Loxton, Howard. *Pilgrimage to Canterbury*. Totowa, N. J.: Rowman & Littlefield, 1978.

Luscombe, D. E. Intro to *Peter Abelard's 'Ethics.'* Oxford: Clarendon Press,1971.

McCracken, S. "Confessional Prologues and the Topography of the Canon's Yeoman." *Modern Philology* 68 (1971): 289–91.

McGuire, Stella. "The Significance of Haukyn, Activa Vita, in *Piers Plowman*." *Review of English Studies* 25 (1949): 97–109.

McNally, John J. "The Penitential and Courtly Traditions in Gower's *Confessio Amantis*." *Studies in Medieval Culture*, edited by John R. Sommerfeldt. Kalamazoo: Western Michigan University Press, 1964. Pp. 74–94.

McNeil, John T. and Gamer, Helena M. "Medicine for Sin as Prescribed in the Penitentials." *Church History* 1 (1932): 14–26.

————. *Medieval Handbooks of Penance.* New York: Columbia University Press, 1938.

Manly, John M. *Some New Light on Chaucer.* New York: Holt, 1926.

———— and Rickart, Edith. *The Text of the Canterbury Tales, Studied on the Basis of All Known Manuscripts.* Vol. 3. Chicago: University of Chicago Press,1940.

Mann, Jill. *Chaucer and Medieval Estates Satire.* Cambridge: Cambridge University Press, 1973.

Martin, Paul. "Sin, Guilt, and Mental Health: Confession and Restitution as Means of Therapy." *Christian Century* 92 (1921): 525–27.

Matthews, William. *The Tragedy of Arthur: A Study of the Alliterative "Morte Arthure."* Berkeley and Los Angeles: University of California Press, 1960.

Miller, Robert P. "Chaucer's Pardoner, the Scriptural Eunuch, and the Pardoner's Tale." *Speculum* 30 (1955): 180–99.

Mitchell, Charles. "The Moral Superiority of Chaucer's Pardoner." *College English* 27, no. 6 (1966): 437–44.

Mooreman, J. H. R. *Church Life in England in the Thirteenth Century.* Cambridge: Cambridge University Press, 1945.

Morris, Colin. *The Discovery of the Individual: 1050–1200.* New York: Harper and Row, 1972.

Muscatine, Charles. *Chaucer and the French Tradition.* 1957; reprint ed. Berkeley: University of California Press, 1973.

Narramore, Bruce. "Guilt: Where Theology and Psychology Meet." *Journal of Psychology and Theology* 2 (1974): 18–25.

New Catholic Encyclopedia. Edited by Conde B. Pallen and John J. Wynne. New York: Universal Knowledge Foundation, 1929.

New Catholic Dictionary. Edited by Conde B. Pallen and John J. Wynn. New York: Universal Knowledge Foundation, 1929.

Outler, A. C. "Karl Menninger and the Dimensions of Sin." *Theology Today* 31 (1974): 59–61.

Owst, George R. *Literature and the Pulpit in Medieval England.* Cambridge: The University Press, 1933.

———. *Preaching in Medieval England.* 1926; reprint ed. New York: Russell & Russell, 1965.

Painter, Sidney. *The Reign of King John.* 1949; reprint ed. Baltimore, Md.: The Johns Hopkins University Press, 1964.

Palmer, P. F. *Sacraments and Forgiveness: Sources of Christian Theology.* Vol. 2. London: Darton, Longman & Todd, 1959.

Panofsky, Erwin. *Early Netherlandish Painting.* New York: Harper & Row, 1953; reprint ed. Icon Editions, 1971.

Pantin, W. A. *The English Church in the Fourteenth Century.* South Bend, Ind.: University of Notre Dame Press, 1962.

Passon, Richard. " 'Entente' in Chaucer's *Friars Tale.*" *Chaucer Review* 2 (1967): 166–71.

Patterson, Lea W. "Chaucerian Confession: Penitential Literature and the Pardoner." *Medievalia et Humanistica: Studies in Medieval and Renaissance Culture,* n.s. 7 (1976): 153–73.

Payen, Jean-Charles *Le Motif du repentir dans la littérature française médiévale.* Geneva: Librairie Droz: 1968.

Peckham, John L. *Archbishop Peckham as a Religious Educator.* New Haven, Conn.: Yale University Press, 1934.

"Penance." *The Catholic Encyclopedia.* 1911 edition.

"Penance." *Sacramentum Mundi: An Encyclopedia of Theology.* Edited by Karl Rahner et al. New York: Herder & Herder, 1968–70.

"Pénitence, la reforme Carolingienne, la pratique." *Dictionnaire de Theologie Catholique.* Vol. 12. Edited by Emile Amann. Paris: Librairie Letouzey et Ane, 1933.

"Penitenceris Apostolique, Histoire." *Dictionnaire de Theologie Catholique.* Vol. 12. Edited by Emile Amann. Paris: Labrairie Letouzey et Ane, 1933.

Pfander, H. G. "Some Medieval Manuals of Religious Instruction in England and Observations on Chaucer's *Parson's Tale.*" *JEGP* 35 (1936): 243–58.

Pirie-Gordon, C. H. C. *Innocent the Great: An Essay on His Life and Times.* London: Longmans, Green & Co., 1907.

"Poenitentiarius." *Glossarium Mediae et Infimae Latinitatus.* Vol. 6.

BIBLIOGRAPHY

Edited by Carolo de Fresne et al. Paris: Librairie des Sciences et des Artes, 1938.

Poschmann, Bernhard. *Penance and the Anointing of the Sick.* Translated by Francis Courtney. New York: Herder & Herder, 1964.

Powell, James M., ed. *Innocent III: Vicar of Christ or Lord of the World?* Boston: D. C. Heath & Co., 1963.

Powicke, Frederick M. "England: Richard I and John." *Cambridge Medieval History.* Vol. 6. New York: Macmillan Co., 1936.

Pratt, R. A. "The Development of the Wife of Bath." In *Studies in Medieval Literature in Honor of Professor Albert Croll Baugh,* pp. 45–79. Philadelphia: University of Pennsylvania Press, 1961.

Riga, P. J. "Penance in St. Ambrose." *Eglise et Théologie* 4 (May 1973): 213–26.

Robertson, D. W. "Frequency of Preaching in Thirteenth Century England." *Speculum* 24 (1949): 376–88.

Rordorf, W. "La Remission des péchés selon la Didache." *Irenikon* 46, no. 3 (1973): 283–97.

Rulter, George M. "Confession in Medieval Literature." Dissertation, Harvard University, 1929.

Russell, Josiah Cox. *Dictionary of Writers of Thirteenth-Century England.* London: Longmans, Green & Co., 1936.

Ryan, Laurence V. "The Canon's Yeoman's Desperate Confession." *Chaucer Review* 8 (1974): 297–310.

Ryan, William M. *William Langland.* New York: Twayne Publishers, 1968.

Sacramentum Mundi: An Encyclopedia of Theology. Edited by Karl Rahner et al. New York: Herder & Herder, 1968–70.

Salu, M. B. Translator's note. *The Ancrene Riwle.* London: Burns & Oates, 1973.

Sayce, Olive. "Chaucer's 'Retractions': The Conclusion of the *Canterbury Tales* and Its Place in Literary Tradition." *MÆ* 40 (1971): 230–48.

Scholes, Robert. *Approaches to the Novel.* San Francisco, Calif.: Chandler Publishing Co., 1966.

Schueler, Donald G. "The Age of the Lover in Gower's *Confessio Amantis.*" *MÆ* 36 (1967): 152–58.

Shedd, Gordon M. "Knight in Tarnished Armour: The Meaning of *Sir Gawain and the Green Knight.*" *Modern Language Review* 62 (1976): 3–13.

Sheehan, M. *Apologetics and Catholic Doctrine.* Dublin: M. H. Gill & Son, Ltd., 1955.

"Sin." *The Catholic Encyclopedia.* 1911 edition.

"Sin, Theology of." *New Catholic Encyclopedia.* 1969 edition.

Smith, Charles E. *Innocent III: Church Defender.* Baton Rouge: Louisiana State University Press, 1961.

Snoeck, Andreas. *Confession and Psychoanalysis.* Westminster, Md.: The Neuman Press, 1964.

Soucy, A. Francis. "Gawain's Fault: 'Angardez Pryde.' " *Chaucer Review* 13 (1978): 166–76.

Southern, R. W. *The Making of the Middle Ages.* 1953; reprint ed. New Haven, Conn.: Yale University Press, 1967.

Spearing, A. C. "*Patience* and the *Gawain*-Poet." *Anglia* 24 (1966): 305–29.

Stevenson, B. "Confession and Psychotherapy." *Journal of Pastoral Care* 20 (1966): 10–15.

Strohm, Paul. "Chaucer's Audience." *Literature and History* 5 (1977): 26–41.

Sumption, Jonathan. *Pilgrimage: An Image of Mediaeval Religion.* Totowa, N. J.: Roman and Littlefield, 1975.

Tentler, Thomas N. *Sin and Confession on the Eve of the Reformation.* Princeton, N. J.: Princeton University Press, 1977.

Thomas, L. B. "Sacramental Confession and Some Clinical Concerns." *Journal of Religion and Health* 4 (1965): 345–53.

Thurston, Fr. Herbert. "The Conversion of Boccaccio and Chaucer." *Studies: An Irish Quarterly Review of Letters, Philosophy, and Science* 25 (1936): 215–25.

Tupper, Frederick. "Chaucer and the Seven Deadly Sins." *PMLA* 29 (1914): 93–128.

Typographical Antiquities Edited by Joseph Ames. Vol. 1. London: Miller, 1810–19.

Ullman, Walter. *The Individual in Medieval Society.* Baltimore, Md.: The Johns Hopkins University Press, 1966.

VanderVelt, James H., and Odenwald, Robert. *Psychiatry and Catholicism*. New York: McGraw Hill, 1952.

Vogel, Cyrille. *Les "Libri Paenitentiales."* Belgium: Brepols, 1978.

Watkins, Oscar D. *A History of Penance*. Vol. 2. New York: Burt Franklin, 1961.

Wells, John E. *Manual of Writings in Middle English*. New Haven, Conn.: Yale University Press, 1916.

"Will." *Catholic Encyclopedia*. 1911 edition.

Worthen, V. "Psychotherapy and Catholic Confession." *Journal of Religion and Health* 13 (1974): 275–84.

Zacher, Christian K. *Curiosity and Pilgrimage: The Literature of Discovery in Fourteenth-Century England*. Baltimore & London: The Johns Hopkins University Press, 1976.

Index

Abelard, Peter, 32, 77; intention in works of, 31–32, 50. *See also Ethics;* "Good Friday: The Third Nocturn"
Age of discretion, 26, 132–33 n
Alain de Lille, 24
Albigensians, 25
Alexander of Stavensby, (bishop), 52–53
Alphabet of Tales, An, 12, 28
Ambrose, Saint, 20, 120
Ancrene Wisse, 45–51, 53, 55
Aquinas, Saint Thomas, 32, 34, 63, 89
Attrition, 34
Augustine, Saint, 30, 131 n; *De vera et falsa poenitentia* attributed to, 29
Aurôlous Liber, 119

Bailly, Harry, 19, 104–7, 116–17; and the Canon's Yeoman, 107–12
Bartholomew of Exeter, 24
Bede, 22, 24

Canon Law, 21, 26, 29
Canon's Yeoman, 19; prologue of, 107–12, 126
Canterbury Tales, 19, 69, 101–27. *See also individual characters and tales*
Characterization, 12, 34–35, 40–41, 44–45, 50–51, 53, 59–60, 81, 100, 112
Chaucer, Geoffrey, 16, 60, 70, 103.

See also Canterbury Tales; individual characters and tales
Chrysostom, Saint John, 68
Circumstances of sin, 16, 35, 37, 38, 70; as characterization, 59; in *Ancrene Wisse,* 45–51; in Canon's Yeoman's prologue, 108–10
Clensyng of Mannes Soule, 29, 41, 75, 76, 82–83, 84, 133 n
Columbanus, Saint, 23, 24
Confessio Amantis, 45, 69, 81–87
Confession, 11, 12, 15, 20–21, 25, 70; to laymen, 13, 29, 133 n; to priests, 13. *See also Omnis utriusque sexus* decree
Contrition, 12, 16, 33–34; in Canon's Yeoman's prologue, 112; in Chaucer's Retraction, 126; in *Cotton Nero A.x,* 100; in Pardoner's prologue, 116; in *Patience,* 89; in *Pearl,* 95; in *Piers Plowman,* 78; in *Purity,* 90
Conversion of the Blessed Apostle Paul, The, 67
Cotton Nero A.x, 69, 100
Cursor Mundi, 28, 61, 83, 85

Dante (*Commedia*), 70–71

Ego, 57, 58, 98, 127
Engin, 12, 42, 129
Ethics, 31–32, 77

Fabliaux, 60
Fourth Lateran Council, 12, 14, 15,

158